Home & Community
Social Behavior Scales
User's Guide

Home & Community Social Behavior Scales User's Guide

by

Kenneth W. Merrell, Ph.D.
University of Oregon

and

Paul Caldarella, Ph.D.
Brigham Young University

Baltimore • London • Sydney

Paul H. Brookes Publishing Co.
Post Office Box 10624
Baltimore, Maryland 21285-0624
USA

www.brookespublishing.com

Copyright © 2002 by Kenneth W. Merrell
All rights reserved.

"Paul H. Brookes Publishing Co." is a registered trademark
of Paul H. Brookes Publishing Co., Inc.

First printing by Paul H. Brookes Publishing Co., Inc., 2008.
First printing by Kenneth W. Merrell, 2002.

Manufactured in the United States of America by
Versa Press, Inc., East Peoria, Illinois.

The case studies described in this book are composites based on the authors' experiences. In all instances, names and identifying details have been changed to protect confidentiality.

Library of Congress Cataloging-in-Publication Data

Merrell, Kenneth W.
   Home and community social behavior scales user's guide / by Kenneth W. Merrell and Paul Caldarella.
     p.   cm.
   Includes bibliographical references.
   ISBN-13: 978-1-55766-991-9 (pbk.)
   ISBN-10: 1-55766-991-0 (pbk.)
   1. Behavioral assessment of children.   I. Caldarella, Paul.   II. Title.

BF723.S62M467 2008
305.23—dc22   2008021183

British Library Cataloguing in Publication data are available from the British Library.

2012   2011   2010   2009   2008

10   9   8   7   6   5   4   3   2   1

CONTENTS

About the Authors ix
Preface xi
Acknowledgments xiii

1 Introduction to the HCSBS 1
   Overview of the HCSBS. 1
      Description. 1
      Unique Features 2
      Purposes 3
      Contents and Organization 3
   Forms of Social Behavior 6
      Social Competence. 6
      Antisocial Behavior 8
      Social Adjustment 9
   Issues in Using Behavior Rating Scales. 10
      General Characteristics 10
      Advantages 11
      Problems. 12
      Recommended Practices 12
   Summary. 14

2 Administration and Scoring Procedures 15
   Completing the Rating Form. 15
      Spanish Language HCSBS Rating Form 16
   User Qualifications 16
      Qualifications for Completing the Rating Form 16

Qualifications for Scoring the Rating Form 17
Qualifications for Interpreting the Results 17
Directions for Scoring the Rating Form 18
Step 1: Calculate Subscale Raw Scores. 18
Step 2: Calculate Total Raw Scores 19
Step 3: Convert Raw Scores to *T*-Scores and Percentile Ranks 19
Step 4: Identify and Record Social Functioning Levels 19
Summary. 20

3 Interpreting and Using HCSBS Scores 21
Three-Level Interpretation Strategy 21
Interpretation Level 1: *T*-Scores and Percentile Ranks 21
Interpretation Level 2: Social Functioning Levels 23
Interpretation Level 3: Qualitative Inspection of Individual Items 26
Case Studies 27
Case Study 1: Jeff 27
Case Study 2: Carrie 29
Cross-Informant Assessment with the HCSBS 31
Using the HCSBS in Functional Behavioral Assessment 32
Linking Assessment to Intervention. 33
Summary. 35

4 Development, Standardization, and Normative Information 37
HCSBS Development Procedures 37
Original Development Procedures for the SSBS. 38
Step 1: Item Development. 38
Step 2: Item Refinement and Reduction 39
Step 3: Content Validation 39
Step 4: Item Rating Format 39
Data Collection Procedures. 40
Characteristics of the Norming Sample 41
Raters 41
Communities, States, and Geographic Regions. 41
Race and Ethnicity. 42

Socioeconomic Status 43
　　　Special Education Participation 45
　　　Age 46
　　　Gender 48
　Development of Score Conversion Tables 50
　　　Development of the Spanish-Language HCSBS Rating Form 50
　Summary 51

5　**Reliability of the HCSBS** 53
　Internal Consistency Reliability 53
　Standard Error of Measurement 54
　Test–Retest Reliability 55
　Interrater Reliability 56
　Summary 58

6　**Validity of the HCSBS** 59
　Evidence Based on Test Content 59
　Evidence Based on Internal Structure 62
　　　Factor Structure 63
　　　Intercorrelations Among HCSBS Scale Scores 65
　Evidence Based on Relations to Other Variables 67
　　　HCSBS and Social Skills Rating System 68
　　　HCSBS and Conners Parent Rating Scale, Revised 69
　　　HCSBS and Child Behavior Checklist 70
　　　HCSBS and Behavioral Assessment System for Children 72
　　　HCSBS and ADHD Symptoms Rating Scale 75
　　　HCSBS and Psychopathy Screening Device 76
　　　Summary of Convergent and Discriminant Validity Studies 77
　Evidence Based on Consequences of Testing 78
　　　Group Differences: At-Risk Status 78
　　　Group Differences: Special Education Status 80
　　　Group Differences: ADHD Clinical Status 81
　　　Group Differences: Gender 83
　Sensitivity to Treatment Outcomes 83

viii CONTENTS

      Outcome Evidence: A Prevention Program 84

      Outcome Evidence: Anger Control Training 85

  Future Research 86

  Summary. 86

References. 87

Appendix A: Score Conversion Tables for Ages 5–11 91

Appendix B: Score Conversion Tables for Ages 12–18. 99

ABOUT THE AUTHORS

Kenneth W. Merrell, Ph.D., is Professor of School Psychology at the University of Oregon, where he has served as School Psychology Program Coordinator and as Head of the Department of Special Education and Clinical Sciences. Dr. Merrell has experience working as a school psychologist in public schools in Oregon and Idaho. He is the author of many journal articles and several books on the topic of social-emotional assessment and intervention with children and youth, as well as the Strong Kids™ social-emotional learning curricula (Paul H. Brookes Publishing Co., 2007). In addition to the Home and Community Social Behavior Scales and School Social Behavior Scales, Second Edition, Dr. Merrell has authored or coauthored several other assessment instruments, including the Preschool and Kindergarten Behavior Scales, Internalizing Symptoms Scale for Children, and ADHD Symptoms Rating Scale. A Fellow of the American Psychological Association, he received his Ph.D. in school psychology from the University of Oregon.

Paul Caldarella, Ph.D., is Director and Research Coordinator of the Positive Behavior Support Initiative in the McKay School of Education at Brigham Young University, where he is also an Adjunct Associate Professor in the Department of Counseling and Special Education. He previously held faculty appointments at Weber State University and Southern Utah University. Dr. Caldarella is author or coauthor of several professional publications and numerous presentations at professional meetings in the fields of education and psychology. A licensed psychologist, he has extensive clinical experience working with at-risk students and their families, including a 1-year internship in child clinical psychology at the University of Arkansas for Medical Sciences, a 1-year fellowship in adolescent clinical psychology at Brown University, and several years experience in private practice settings. Dr. Caldarella received his Ph.D. in combined professional-scientific psychology from Utah State University in 1998, an M.S. in counseling psychology from Utah State University in 1995, and a B.A. in psychology and philosophy from Rhode Island College in 1988.

PREFACE

A convincing body of evidence has accumulated regarding the importance of social competence and the problems associated with antisocial behavior in children and youth. Stated simply, young people who fail to develop adequate social competencies, or who engage in antisocial behaviors to a significant extent, are in danger of severe negative outcomes, which may fundamentally alter the course of their lives and their chances for success and adjustment. The ramifications of failure to develop adequate levels of social competence include, among other things, peer rejection, depression and anxiety, underemployment and unemployment, mental health problems, inadequate social support, and unsatisfactory interpersonal and familial relations. The ramifications of engaging in significant antisocial behavior during the formative years include involvement with the justice system, employment problems, substance abuse and mental health problems, strained interpersonal and family relationships, perpetration of child and spouse abuse, and the continuation of this cycle to the next generation through an insidious pattern of modeling and coercion. When severe deficits in social competence occur simultaneously with high levels of antisocial behavior (which is often the case), the prognosis is particularly grim. Although these problems are not particularly rare, their costs to individuals, families, and society are enormous.

Fortunately there are a growing collection of proven techniques and programs for prevention and treatment of social competence deficits and antisocial behavior. Although it is not necessarily easy to create substantive positive change in social and antisocial behavior, it can be done. There are school systems and community agencies nationwide and worldwide that are adapting the available prevention and intervention technology to their specific circumstances to effect important social-behavioral outcomes. Sometimes these changes occur one child at a time, and sometimes they occur on a schoolwide or agencywide basis. Either way, effective prevention and treatment of social behavior problems can significantly improve the adjustment and life outcomes for children and youth.

Screening and assessment provides the basis for effective intervention. Without reliable and valid screening procedures, it is not possible to identify accurately the specific children and youth who should be targeted for prevention and intervention efforts, nor is it possible to identify the specific clusters of social-behavioral deficits or problems that should be the focus of prevention and intervention efforts. In sum, the availability and use of practical, easy-to-use, low-cost, reliable, and valid measurement tools for social-behavioral concerns are prerequisites to making positive change.

The Home and Community Social Behavior Scales (HCSBS) is a screening and assessment tool that meets all of these criteria. This instrument is a 64-item behavior rating scale designed to be completed by parents and other home-based raters of children and youth ages 5–18. It simultaneously provides a reliable and valid measure of both social competence and antisocial behavior. The HCSBS is a companion instrument to the School Social Behavior Scales, Second Edition (SSBS-2), which is similar to the HCSBS but designed to be used by educators to rate the social and antisocial behavior of students in school settings. Together, the HCSBS and SSBS-2 form the Social Behavior Scales, a cross-informant system for screening and assessing social competence and antisocial behavior of children and youth.

The HCSBS is a practical and easy to use. The items on the HCSBS depict routine or commonly occurring social competencies and antisocial behavior problems of children and youth. The rating form takes only a few minutes to complete and includes a built-in simple scoring key. Other than the rating forms and User's Guides, no special equipment or materials are needed to complete and score the HCSBS or the SSBS-2. The level of training needed to use the HCSBS effectively is minimal. This User's Guide contains complete and simple instructions for administering, scoring, and interpreting the HCSBS. It also includes recommendations for using the HCSBS in decision-making and intervention planning, as well as detailed evidence regarding the tool's reliability and validity.

Chapter 1 provides an introduction to the HCSBS. Included in this chapter is an overview and description of the scales, an informative discussion regarding forms of social behavior in children and youth, and an analysis of some of the major issues in using behavior rating scales such as the HCSBS and SSBS-2 for screening and assessing children and adolescents.

Chapter 2 includes detailed yet easy-to-follow instructions for administering and scoring the HCSBS. Qualifications for users of the scales are explained, and the easy four-step process for scoring the rating form is outlined.

Chapter 3 provides a guide to interpreting and using HCSBS scores. A straightforward three-level interpretation strategy is suggested, and the use of this strategy is illustrated with two detailed case studies. This chapter also provides guidelines for using the HCSBS along with the SSBS-2 for cross-informant social-behavioral assessment of children and youth, using the HCSBS as an initial component of functional behavioral assessment, and linking assessment data to intervention planning.

Chapters 4, 5, and 6 form the "technical manual" portion of the guide. The first three chapters are essential for routine use of the scales, whereas the final three chapters provide extensive details regarding the development of the scales and the norming samples, as well as psychometric evidence in support of the reliability and validity of the HCSBS. Although Chapters 4, 5, and 6 are not essential for routine use of the scales, they are absolutely essential to document the integrity of the scales and to compare them against the highest standard for educational and psychological assessment instruments. All users of the HCSBS are encouraged to become familiar with the technical aspects of the HCSBS, which have been carefully detailed in the final three chapters of the User's Guide. A careful review of this technical information will aid users in better understanding the constructs measured by the HCSBS and the purposes for which it is has been validated. A careful examination of the technical information should convince users of the HCSBS that it meets the very highest standards of technically adequacy and that they may use these scales with great confidence for screening and assessing social competence and antisocial behavior of children and youth.

ACKNOWLEDGMENTS

Development and refinement of the Home and Community Social Behavior Scales (HCSBS) has been an ongoing process over the past several years. An effort of this magnitude cannot be done alone. I am indebted to many individuals and several institutions critical to the successful culmination of this project and the acceptance the scales have received among professionals in schools, clinics, and social service agencies. In addition, I appreciate greatly the efforts of all the individuals who provided ratings of children and adolescents for the HCSBS norming sample and related research or who coordinated data collection efforts.

I wish to thank my coauthor, Dr. Paul Caldarella. It was his interest and enthusiasm for field testing a parent rating version of the School Social Behavior Scales that spurred me on to undertake the first studies of the HCSBS. Paul's doctoral dissertation in psychology at Utah State University was the first formal effort to investigate the HCSBS, and his efforts were critical in coordinating important early research projects involving the scales in Utah, Arkansas, and Rhode Island. I also wish to thank my colleague Dr. Susan Crowley of Utah State University for her statistical analyses and methodological advice that was critical in developing the subscale structure of the HCSBS.

The Iowa Measurement Research Foundation (IMRF) under the leadership of Dr. Leonard Feldt at the University of Iowa provided financial support for a first large wave of data collection with the HCSBS at the national level from 1999 through 2001, as well as the initial psychometric analyses. The IMRF business manager, George Karr, was always helpful and prompt in assisting me with the many logistical and fiscal details that had to be dealt with during these efforts. I appreciate greatly their support and assistance.

During my 4 years at the University of Iowa, when a great deal of the HCSBS research was initiated, I was fortunate to have the assistance of several graduate students who became involved with the project. I am especially grateful for the efforts of Dr. Angela Streeter, Dr. Eric Boelter, and Jackie Lund, who worked hard on various aspects of the project and who all coauthored HCSBS research articles with me.

In addition, there are a large number of individuals and institutions that were of assistance during the HCSBS norming and validation research, in developing the Spanish language version of the scales, and in various other efforts to promote and disseminate the scales. Specifically, I express my sincere appreciation to the following, in no particular order: Rebecca Foster, Betty Heller, Mary Lou Darczuk, Larry Stinn, Randy Krejci, Nancy Brown, Jackie Bofford, Carl Cason, Pili Wolfe, Jeanie Engelland, Brad Moon, Virginia Latta, Mitchell Prinstein, Kimberly Kobus, John

Boekamp, Lex Grapentine, Dr. Patricia Youngdahl, Dr. Abesie Kelly, Dr. Glen White, Dr. Richard West, Dr. Richard Young, Dr. Deanna Sanders, Dr. Karen Snyder, Todd McFarland, Amanda Gentry, Dr. Dianna Carrizales, Dr. Sara Castro-Olivo, Adam Fisher, Isaac Adams, Susan Merrell, Susan Mielke, and Hugh Pyle.

Thanks to the staff at Paul H. Brookes Publishing Co. for their interest in taking over the publication and distribution of the HCSBS and the School Social Behavior Scales, Second Edition (SSBS-2) and for their commitment to improving children's education and mental health through their publishing business. Again, thanks to all those who have provided assistance throughout the very long and complicated process that has led to this publication of the HCSBS rating forms and User's Guide. It is my hope that professionals who use the HCSBS and the SSBS-2 will find these tools to be practical, easy to use, and helpful in serving the educational and mental health needs of children and youth.

INTRODUCTION TO THE HCSBS   1

This introductory chapter describes the Home and Community Social Behavior Scales (HCSBS) and the need for assessment and intervention of social and antisocial behavior of children and youth. Dimensions of social and antisocial behavior are discussed, as are relationships among these constructs. In addition, subsequent chapters of this manual pertain to administration and scoring (Chapter 2), interpretation and use of scores (Chapter 3), development and normative information (Chapter 4), reliability data (Chapter 5), and validity evidence for the HCSBS (Chapter 6).

OVERVIEW OF THE HCSBS

This section provides basic information about the HCSBS scales. The scales are described, unique features are listed, purposes are delineated, and their contents and organization are discussed.

Description

The HCSBS is a behavior rating scale designed for use in evaluating social competence and antisocial behavior of children and youth ages 5–18. It is a norm-referenced, standardized assessment developed for use by parents and other home-based raters (e.g., grandparents, guardians, group home supervisors). Separate normative information and score conversion tables are provided for children and youth ages 5–11 and 12–18. The HCSBS is a companion instrument to the School Social Behavior Scales, Second Edition (SSBS-2; Merrell, 2002). Together, these instruments comprise the Social Behavior Scales, a cross-informant system for evaluating the social and antisocial behavior of children and youth across school, home, and community settings. The HCSBS and the SSBS-2 are conceptually similar, contain the same number of items, and include similar item content, rating formats, and score conversion systems. The SSBS-2, however, was designed for use by educators based on social and antisocial behavior in school settings, whereas the HCSBS was designed for use by home-based raters, based on social and antisocial behavior in home and community settings.

The HCSBS includes 64 items in two major scales—*Social Competence* (Scale A) and *Antisocial Behavior* (Scale B)—each consisting of 32 items. Both of these scales are composed of empirically derived subscales that are useful in identifying specific clusters or domains of social and antisocial behavior. The Social Competence scale includes items that describe positive social skills and traits that are characteristic of well-adjusted and socially skilled children and youth. The Antisocial Behavior scale includes items that describe various socially related problem behaviors that may impede socialization, be destructive or harmful to others, and produce negative social outcomes.

Unique Features

Clinicians and researchers who have a need to use child behavior rating scales for screening and assessment purposes have a wide array of alternatives from which to choose. There are many technically adequate behavior rating scales that have proven to be useful for evaluating child and adolescent behavior. The HCSBS and SSBS-2 social behavior rating scales, however, offer some unique advantages. In making a decision regarding which behavior rating scale to use, consider the following unique features of the Social Behavior Scales:

- These instruments were developed specifically for screening and assessing the social and antisocial behavior of children and youth and are based on current theory and research in this domain. Thus, the HCSBS and SSBS-2 have a specific and unique focus on social functioning.

- The HCSBS and SSBS-2 focus on typical, general, and routine social competencies and antisocial problem behaviors of children and youth that are commonly manifested in home, community, and school settings. Many other child behavior rating instruments are highly clinical in nature and include items that reflect significant psychopathology or psychiatric symptoms. Although the HCSBS and SSBS-2 have been shown to be useful for assessing children with significant behavior, social, emotional, and developmental problems, their main emphasis is on routine or commonly occurring social competencies and problems. Parents and professionals who rate the behavior of children or youth using the HCSBS or SSBS-2 will be comfortable with the terminology and behavioral descriptors used and are not likely to be confused or offended by items describing extremely low incidence severe behavior characteristics.

- Because the HCSBS and SSBS-2 are companion instruments, they comprise a cross-informant rating system useful for screening and assessing social and antisocial behavior of children and youth across a range of settings and from the perspective of a variety of behavioral informants.

- These instruments are brief enough to be completed in only a few minutes but comprehensive and focused enough to provide a detailed and thorough screening of social and antisocial behavior.

- The HCSBS rating forms are available in both English and Spanish language versions. Availability in Spanish is an increasingly essential feature of child assessment systems because the proportion of the U.S. population whose primary language is Spanish has increased rapidly since the 1990s.

Purposes

Although useful for a wide variety of circumstances and objectives, the Social Behavior Scales were developed to be used specifically for the following purposes:

- Screening tools for identifying children and youth who are behaviorally at risk and who may benefit from prevention or intervention efforts
- Components of a *multimethod, multisource, multisetting assessment design* (Merrell, 2008) for identifying, classifying, and determining service eligibility for children and youth with significant social skills deficits and antisocial behavior problems
- Tools for assessing social skills deficiencies and antisocial behavior problems for the purpose of developing appropriate interventions
- Measurement instruments for monitoring child and adolescent behavior change or responsiveness during the course of an intervention, as well as for evaluation of the effectiveness of the intervention
- Research instruments for studying the social behavior characteristics and patterns of children and youth

Contents and Organization

The contents and organization of the HCSBS were designed to provide a comprehensive yet concise sampling of the behaviors and characteristics within the domains of social competence and antisocial behavior. The HCSBS items were derived from the first edition of its companion measure, the original SSBS, which was designed based on the same premises. To specifically adapt the SSBS items to make them relevant for use in home and community rather than school settings, several of the items were reworded slightly to reflect home and community contexts rather than educational contexts. For example, the SSBS items *Follows school and classroom rules* and *Invites other students to participate in activities* were reworded to *Follows family and community rules* and *Invites peers to participate in activities*, respectively. Within the social competence domain, items for the SSBS and HCSBS were developed to reflect the important subdomains of peer-related social adjustment, adult-related social adjustment, and self-related social adjustment. Within the antisocial behavior domain, items were developed to be consistent with current theory and research regarding development and manifestation of both covert and overt forms of antisocial behavior.

Social Competence Scale The HCSBS Social Competence scale (Scale A) includes 32 items that describe adaptive or positive behaviors that are likely to lead to positive personal and social outcomes. These items are rated using a five-point scale on which the anchor points range from 1 = Never to 5 = Frequently. The items in the Social Competence scale are divided into two empirically derived subscales, described as follows.

The *Peer Relations* subscale includes 17 items that reflect behavior characteristics important in making friends, being a positive and constructive member of a peer group, and being well liked by other children or youth. The items in this subscale are linked most strongly to the peer-related form of social adjustment. Examples of items in the Peer Relations subscale include *Cooperates with peers, Will give in or compromise with peers when appropriate, Interacts with a wide variety of peers, Has good leadership skills*, and *Is "looked up to" or respected by peers*.

The *Self-Management/Compliance* subscale includes 15 items that reflect behaviors and characteristics that are important in responding to the social expectations of parents, teachers, and other influential adults in a child or adolescent's life, such as work supervisors, religious leaders, coaches, youth group leaders, and so forth. The items within this subscale are linked strongly to both the adult-related and self-related forms of social adjustment because they characterize behaviors that are important in complying with appropriate expectations of adults as well as showing appropriate self-restraint and self-management. Examples of items in the Self-Management/Compliance subscale include *Completes chores without being reminded, Follows family and community rules, Responds appropriately when corrected by parents or supervisors*, and *Shows self-control*. The items of the HCSBS Social Competence scale are shown in Table 1.1, presented by the subscale to which they are assigned.

Antisocial Behavior Scale The HCSBS Antisocial Behavior scale (Scale B) includes 32 items that describe common socially related behavior problems of children and youth. These behaviors are considered to be antisocial in nature because they are directed at others; may lead to delinquency; or are likely to lead to negative social consequences such as peer rejection, strained relations with peers, or strained relations with parents, teachers, or other adults. The problem behavior characteristics reflected by items in this scale include a combination of overt and covert antisocial behaviors. Overt antisocial behaviors are those that are easily observed by others, reflected by such items as *Has temper outbursts or tantrums, Swears or uses offensive language*, or *Threatens others; is verbally aggressive*. Covert antisocial behaviors are those that may be enacted in secret without the immediate knowledge of others, such as the items *Takes things that are not his or hers, Destroys or damages others' property*, and *Cheats on schoolwork or in games*. Like the items in the HCSBS Social Competence scale, the items from the Antisocial Behavior scale are rated using a five-point scale on which the anchor points range from 1 = Never to 5 = Frequently. These items are divided into two empirically derived subscales.

Table 1.1. Items in the HCSBS Social Competence scale, listed by subscale

Peer Relations
1. Cooperates with peers
4. Offers help to peers when needed
5. Participates effectively in family or group activities
6. Understands problems and needs of peers
9. Invites peers to participate in activities
11. Has skills or abilities that are admired by peers
12. Is accepting of peers
15. Will give in or compromise with peers when appropriate
19. Interacts with a wide variety of peers
21. Is good at initiating or joining conversations with peers
22. Is sensitive to the feelings of others
25. Enters appropriately into ongoing activities with peers
26. Has good leadership skills
28. Notices and compliments accomplishments of others
29. Is assertive in an appropriate way when he or she needs to be
30. Is invited by peers to join in activities
32. Is "looked up to" or respected by peers

Self-Management/Compliance
2. Makes appropriate transitions between different activities
3. Completes chores without being reminded
7. Remains calm when problems arise
8. Listens to and carries out directions from parents or supervisors
10. Asks appropriately for clarification of instructions
13. Completes chores or other assigned tasks independently
14. Completes chores or other assigned tasks on time
16. Follows family and community rules
17. Behaves appropriately at school
18. Asks for help in an appropriate manner
20. Produces work of acceptable quality for his or her ability level
23. Responds appropriately when corrected by parents or supervisors
24. Controls temper when angry
27. Adjusts to different behavioral expectations across settings
31. Shows self-control

The *Defiant/Disruptive* subscale includes 15 items that are indicative of an oppositional, explosive, and "in your face" pattern of behavior. Children and youth who engage in high rates of these behaviors are likely to be seen as pushy, belligerent, challenging, oppositional, irritable, and unpredictable. They tend to draw attention to themselves by disrupting ongoing activities and challenging adults who are in positions of authority. The behavior characteristics reflected in the items of this subscale are incompatible with both peer-related and adult-related forms of social adjustment and are primarily overt in nature. These behavior characteristics bear some similarity to the symptoms of *oppositional defiant disorder* from the *Diagnostic and Statistical Manual of Mental Disorders, Fourth Edition, Text Revision* (DSM-IV-TR; American Psychiatric Association, 2000). Examples of items in the Defiant/Disruptive subscale include *Bothers and annoys others*, *Is defiant to parents or supervisors*, and *Has temper outbursts or tantrums*.

The *Antisocial/Aggressive* subscale includes 17 items that are indicative of a pattern of coercive behavior; a lack of empathy; violation of family, community, and school rules; dishonesty; and threatening or menacing behavior. Children and youth who engage in high rates of these behaviors are seen as dangerous, destructive, mean, and shrewd. They are often seen as being calculated, callous, and only looking out for themselves. If these behaviors are severe and go unchecked, they may lead to a long-term pattern of antisocial behavior and trouble with the law. The behavior characteristics reflected in these 17 items are incompatible with both peer-related and adult-related forms of social adjustment and may be overt or covert in nature. These characteristics are generally compatible with the symptoms of *conduct disorder* from the DSM-IV-TR. Examples of items in the Antisocial/Aggressive subscale include *Disregards feelings or needs of others*, *Destroys or damages others' property*, and *Is cruel to other persons or to animals*. The items of the HCSBS Antisocial Behavior scale are shown in Table 1.2, divided by the subscales.

FORMS OF SOCIAL BEHAVIOR

Since about the early 1980s, researchers in the fields of child psychology and education have made substantial progress in the articulation of a *behavioral dimensions* approach to classifying the competencies and problem behaviors of children and youth (Caldarella & Merrell, 1997; Kauffman, 2000; Merrell, 2008). The behavioral dimensions approach differs substantially from traditional medical models of "behavior as disease" because specific behavior characteristics of children and youth are only considered to belong to the same dimension or domain after they have been proven to cluster or factor together through the use of sophisticated multivariate statistical techniques, such as factor analysis, cluster analysis, and structural equation modeling. The HCSBS and SSBS-2 reflect the behavioral dimensions approach in their articulation of scales and subscales of social and antisocial behavior. The results of the factor analytic procedures used in developing the HCSBS scales are presented in Chapter 6.

The initial development of items and scales of the HCSBS and original SSBS were developed through careful consideration of theoretical models of social and antisocial behavior, as well as forms of social adjustment. Therefore, the items of these instruments reflect a rational-theoretical approach to their development as well as the behavioral dimensions model. This section provides a brief overview of the theory and research on which the primary constructs measured by the HCSBS and SSBS contents are based.

Social Competence

Social competence is a complex, multidimensional construct that has been defined a variety of ways in the literature. A proposed cognitive definition of

Table 1.2. Items in HCSBS Antisocial Behavior scale, listed by subscale

Defiant/Disruptive
1. Blames others for his or her problems
3. Is defiant to parents or supervisors
6. Is dishonest; tells lies
8. Is disrespectful or "sassy"
9. Is easily provoked; has a "short fuse"
10. Ignores parents or supervisors
14. Has temper outbursts or tantrums
16. Is overly demanding of attention from adults
21. Whines and complains
23. Is difficult to control
24. Bothers and annoys others
28. Is not dependable
30. Acts impulsively without thinking
31. Is easily irritated
32. Demands help from peers

Antisocial/Aggressive
2. Takes things that are not his or hers
4. Cheats on schoolwork or in games
5. Gets into fights
7. Teases and makes fun of others
11. Acts as if he or she is better than others
12. Destroys or damages others' property
13. Will not share with others
15. Disregards feelings or needs of others
17. Threatens others; is verbally aggressive
18. Swears or uses offensive language
19. Is physically aggressive
20. Insults peers
22. Argues or quarrels with peers
25. Gets into trouble at school or in the community
26. Disrupts ongoing activities
27. Boasts and brags
29. Is cruel to other persons or to animals

social competence by Meichenbaum, Butler, and Gruson (1981) maintained that it includes the components of overt behaviors, cognitive processes, and cognitive structures. Foster and Ritchey (1979) proposed a more behavioral definition of *social competence* and referred to it as "those responses which, within a given situation, maximize the probability of producing, maintaining, or enhancing positive effects for the interactor" (p. 626). Given that the assessment of social competence by means of behavior rating scales produces a rather distinct, if not narrow, picture of the construct, a more pragmatic, functional definition appears to be useful. In this regard, the authors of the HCSBS concur with a definition of *social competence* provided by Hops (1983), who referred to it as "a summary term which reflects social judgment about the general quality of an individual's performance in a given situation" (p. 3). Thus, social competence is best viewed as a broad construct that may involve judgments about specific social behaviors but is focused primarily on how an individual's adaptive social behavior characteristics are viewed in general (Merrell, 2008; Merrell & Gimpel, 1998).

Social competence is closely related to two other constructs, namely, social skills and social acceptance or rejection. *Social skills* are considered to be a subdomain of the construct of social competence and are defined as specific behavior skills used to respond in given social situations (Gresham, 1986; Gresham & Reschly, 1987; Merrell & Gimpel, 1998). *Social acceptance* and *social rejection* reflect one's social status with peers and usually are measured through sociometric assessments (Landau & Milich, 1990; Merrell, 2008). Although one might think of social acceptance or rejection as a product or outcome of social competence, it also has been conceptualized as a subdomain of the broader construct of social competence (Gresham & Reschly, 1987).

The development of adequate social competence during childhood has been found to be a critical factor not only for important outcomes in childhood but also in later success and adjustment in life. Whereas adequate social competence provides an important foundation that generally leads to solid peer relationships (Asher & Taylor, 1981; Merrell & Gimpel, 1998) and academic success (Walker & Hops, 1976), inadequate social competence during childhood has been associated with a number of negative outcomes, including juvenile delinquency (Loeber, 1985), mental health problems (Cowen, Pederson, Babigan, Izzo, & Trost, 1973), conduct-related discharge from military service (Roff, Sells, & Golden, 1972), and the development of antisocial behavior patterns (Dodge, Coie, & Brakke, 1982; Walker, Gresham, & Ramsey, 2004).

Antisocial Behavior

Antisocial behavior has been defined as behavior that impedes adequate socialization, is destructive and harmful, and produces negative social outcomes (Walker et al., 2004). *Antisocial problem behaviors*, as defined in this manual, either have an antisocial component (disregard for the rights or property of others) or lead directly to negative social outcomes, such as peer rejection, delinquency, and incarceration. Because the focus of the HCSBS and SSBS-2 is on social behavior, other classes of problem behavior that are not explicitly social in nature are not addressed in the instrument and should be assessed using other measures if they are a concern. Examples of other types of problem behaviors include hyperactivity, self-stimulation or self-injury, and internalizing problems such as depression and anxiety.

It is presumed that antisocial behavior is linked to social competence; however, it is incorrect to think that these two constructs are merely polar opposites. It has been demonstrated that inadequate social competence is associated with higher levels of problematic social behaviors. Gresham and Elliott (1990) contended that socially related problem behaviors interfere with social skills performance, but the nature of the relationship between the two constructs is complex. It is logical to assume that increases in one of the constructs will be associated with decreases in the other, and it is true that this type of relationship has been consistently identified through research; however, there are some well-known exceptions to this notion. Some youth who engage in substantial rates of delinquent, harmful, and destructive antisocial behaviors may also exhibit solid social skills and be perceived as leaders. In a highly influential study of the dimensions and types of social status of youth, Coie, Dodge, and Cappotelli (1982) referred to youth who were perceived to be disruptive, defiant, and hostile, while at the same time showing good leadership skills and being well-liked by some peers as *controversial*. There are other exceptions to the notion that poor social skills and high rates of antisocial behavior go hand-in-hand. For example, some children and adolescents may be withdrawn, shy, reticent, and generally show poor peer-related social skills, yet they seldom exhibit any antisocial problem behaviors. Coie et al. (1982) referred to such children as *neglected*.

The constructs of social competence and antisocial behavior are definitely linked, but the exact direction and nature of the linkage is sometimes tenuous. Therefore, assessing one of the two domains separately and then inferring the probable level of the other domain based on this assessment may result in unreliable and invalid conclusions. A more defensible practice would be to assess both domains separately, which is why the HCSBS and SSBS-2 include major scales for each domain.

Social Adjustment

It already has been stated that the HCSBS and SSBS-2 were designed to measure both positive social behaviors (social competence) and negative social behaviors (antisocial behavior). In developing these instruments, another behavioral division was also considered, that of *adult-related* versus *peer-related* social adjustment. These two categories reflect the two major types of social-behavioral adjustments that children must make when they enter the school setting (Walker, McConnell, & Clarke, 1985). In school settings, the adult-related form of social adjustment is referred to as *teacher-related* social adjustment. Teacher-related adjustment involves meeting the expectations of teachers within the instructional setting, along with related constraints such as school rules. At a more general level, adult-related adjustment involves meeting the expectations of adults who are in authority, such as parents, caregivers, and supervisors. Peer-related adjustment involves the dynamics of developing appropriate social relationships with other children and youth. Although the types of behaviors likely to facilitate these two basic forms of adjustment have considerable overlap, some researchers have argued that each form of adjustment is somewhat autonomous and that each makes unique contributions to the overall process of social development (e.g., Connolly, 1983; Mueller, 1979). In addition to these two domains of social adjustment, the items of the SSBS-2 were developed to include some coverage of a third domain, *self-related social adjustment*. This form of adjustment may overlap to some extent with teacher-related and peer-related social adjustment but is considered to be an important construct in its own right because it involves self-regulation and self-management skills that are important in ensuring positive social outcomes.

The HCSBS and SSBS-2 were designed to tap both peer-related and adult-related forms of social adjustment. This representation of forms of adjustment did not occur by creating separate scales, as was done to assess both social competence and antisocial behavior. Rather, within each of the two major scales, the content of the items was developed to balance the number of behavioral descriptors that might be linked more closely with one form of adjustment or the other. In addition, the items of the Antisocial Behavior scale were constructed to provide a balance of covert and overt antisocial behaviors.

ISSUES IN USING BEHAVIOR RATING SCALES

This section describes some of the important issues in using behavior rating scales for assessing children and adolescents. Specifically, general characteristics of behavior rating scales, advantages of using behavior rating scales, problems associated with using behavior rating scales, and recommended practices in using behavior rating scales are discussed.

General Characteristics

Behavior rating scales such as the HCSBS and SSBS-2 provide a standardized format for the development of summary judgments about a child or adolescent's behavior characteristics. These judgments are made by an informant who knows the child well. In the case of the HCSBS, the informant should be a parent, guardian, caregiver, or supervisor. With the SSBS-2, the informant or rater should be a teacher or other educator who knows the child or adolescent well.

As an assessment methodology, behavior rating scales are less direct than either direct behavioral observation or structured behavioral interviewing because they are measures of *perceptions* regarding specified behaviors rather than firsthand measures of the behavior. Rating scales, however, are considered to be a direct and objective assessment method and to yield data that are more reliable than either unstructured clinical interviewing or projective techniques (Merrell, 2008). When behavior rating scales began to become more widely used during the 1970s and 1980s, they were often viewed with suspicion and used as a last resort by behaviorally oriented clinicians, but as the research base has increased and technical characteristics have improved, their use has been more broadly accepted. This increased acceptance has occurred as a result of improvements in the evidence base for using behavior rating scales and not just because of a shift in professional opinion.

Conners and Werry (1979) defined *rating scales* as an "algebraic summation, over variable periods of time and numbers of social situations, of many discrete observations" (p. 341). The term *algebraic* indicates that for each rating scale item, various rating choices are available, each of which symbolize a particular level of behavior. An additive checklist, on the other hand, is a list of symptoms or characteristics that the rater checks if present and then obtains a total score of the number of items checked. In general, the algebraic format provided by rating scales is preferred to the simple additive format provided by checklists because it allows for more precise measurement of behavioral frequency or intensity.

Advantages

The widespread popularity of using behavior rating scales is not incidental because these tools offer many advantages for clinicians and researchers who conduct child and adolescent behavioral assessments. The main advantages of behavior rating scales that have been proposed by Merrell (2000a, 2000b, 2008) are summarized as follows:

- In comparison with direct behavioral observation and behavioral interviewing of parents and teachers, behavior rating scales are less expensive in terms of professional time involved and amount of training required to utilize the assessment system.

- Behavior rating scales are capable of providing information on low frequency but important behaviors that might not be seen in direct observation sessions. An example that serves to illustrate this point is a physical attack by one child toward another. In most cases, this type of behavior does not occur on a constant or consistent schedule and might be missed within the constraints of conducting two brief observations. Nonetheless, to know about the occurrence of such behaviors is extremely important.

- As mentioned previously, behavior rating scales are an objective assessment method that provides data that are more reliable and valid than the information provided by unstructured interviews or projective-expressive techniques.

- Behavior rating scales may be used to assess children and youth who cannot readily provide reliable or detailed information about themselves.

- Rating scales capitalize on observations over a period of time in a child or adolescent's natural environment (e.g., the school and home settings). Experienced clinicians understand that there may be problems associated with making a single observation of a child or youth in an environment that is unusual to him or her, such as a clinic or office. Younger children are especially reactive to novel surroundings and their environments in general, and the behavior that they may exhibit in a single session in an unfamiliar setting may not be very representative of their behavior.

- Rating scales capitalize on the judgments and observations of individuals who are highly familiar with the child or adolescent's behavior, such as parents or teachers. These informants are thus considered to be "experts" in their ability to describe a child's behavior, and the information that they provide is usually critical to the assessment process.

Because of these advantages, it is easy to see why rating scales are widely used—they get at the "big picture" in a short amount of time, at moderate cost, and with a substantial amount of validity.

Problems

Despite their many advantages, rating scales have some potential problems. The most sophisticated rating scales available can help provide objective, reliable, and socially valid information, but the nature of rating scale technology has some inherent shortcomings.

The measurement problems of behavior rating scales can be grouped into two classes: *bias of response* and *error variance.* Bias of response refers to the way that informants completing the rating scales may create additional error by the way in which they use the scales. Response bias has three specific types: 1) *halo effects,* rating a child in a positive manner because he or she possesses some other positive characteristic not pertinent to the rated item; 2) leniency or severity effects, the tendency of some raters to have an overly generous or overly critical response set for all of their ratings; and 3) *central tendency effects,* the tendency of raters to select mid-point ratings and to avoid endpoints of the scale such as "never" or "always."

Error variance is closely related to and often overlaps with response bias as a form of rating scale measurement problems but provides a more general representation of some of the problems encountered with this form of assessment. Four types of variance that may create error in the obtained results of a rating scale assessment have been identified. *Source variance* refers to the subjectivity of the rater. *Setting variance* occurs as a result of the situational specificity of behavior, given that humans tend to behave somewhat differently across situations and settings. *Temporal variance* refers to the tendency of behavior ratings to be only moderately consistent over time—partly due to changes in the observed behavior over time and partly due to changes in the rater's approach to the rating task over time. Finally, *instrument variance* refers to the fact that different rating scales measure often related but slightly differing hypothetical constructs (e.g., aggressive behavior vs. delinquent behavior), and a severe problem behavior score on one scale may be compared with only a moderate problem behavior score on a differing rating scale for the same person. Related to instrument variance is the fact that differing assessment tools have their own unique norming samples with which to make score comparisons. If these samples are not representative of the population as a whole, similar scores on two different rating scales may not mean the same thing.

Recommended Practices

Problems associated with using behavior rating scales can be minimized in several ways. Four specific recommended ways of using rating scales, which have been previously proposed by Merrell (2000a, 2008), are discussed next.

1. Use behavior rating scales routinely for early screening and identification.

Effective screening practices involve identifying with a high degree of accuracy children or youth who are in the early stages of developing behavior, social, or emotional problems. The identified children are then evaluated more carefully to determine whether their social behavior problems warrant special program eligibility and intervention services. Screening for social behavior problems is usually done for the purpose of *secondary prevention*, which is the prevention of the existing problem becoming worse (Kauffman, 2000). Screening for early intervention is one of the best uses of behavior rating scales, as they cover a wide variety of important behaviors and take very little time to administer and score.

2. Use the *aggregation principle*.

This principle involves obtaining ratings from a variety of sources, each of which might present a slightly differing picture. When using rating scales for purposes other than routine screening, obtaining aggregated rating scale data is recommended in order to reduce bias of response and variance problems in the assessment. In practice, using aggregated measures means to obtain rating evaluations from different raters in different settings and to use more than one type of rating scale.

3. Use a multimethod, multisource, multisetting assessment design.

When behavior rating scales such as the HCSBS and SSBS-2 are used for formal assessment and decision-making purposes rather than initial screening purposes, they should be used only as one part of a comprehensive assessment design. The same could be said for any other method of child behavioral assessment, whether it be direct behavioral observation, interviews, sociometric techniques, or something else. Because each method of behavioral assessment is subject to certain limitations, it is always best to use a combination or methods, across settings, and with a variety of informant sources to help to obtain a comprehensive picture of the child's functioning and to overcome the limitations of any single method, source, or setting. This type of design has been referred to previously as a *multimethod, multisource, multisetting assessment design* (Merrell, 2008).

4. Use behavior rating scales to monitor intervention progress and outcome.

Kerr and Nelson (1989) demonstrated that continuous assessment and monitoring of student progress following the initial assessment and intervention is very important in successful implementation of behavioral interventions. Progress toward behavioral intervention goals may be assessed easily on a weekly or biweekly schedule using appropriate rating scales. Although rating scales may not be the best measurement choice for gathering daily assessment data, there are a number of other simple ways of assessing progress daily, such as using performance records or brief observational data. Progress monitoring is a critical element of using a *response-to-intervention* method for assessing and supporting students.

Additional assessment following the intervention can also be a useful process. The main reason for follow-up assessment is to determine how well the intervention effects have been maintained over time (e.g., after 3 months) and how well the behavior changes have generalized to other settings (e.g., the home setting and other classrooms). In actual practice, a follow-up assessment might involve having teacher(s) and parent(s) complete behavior rating scales on a child after a specified time period has elapsed following the child's participation in a social skills training program. The data obtained from this follow-up assessment can be used to determine whether follow-up interventions seem appropriate. They may also be useful in developing future intervention programs if social-behavioral gains are not being maintained over time or generalized across specific settings.

SUMMARY

The HCSBS is a unique and practical behavior rating scale designed to be used for screening and assessment of social competence and antisocial behavior of children and youth ages 5–18. This instrument was designed primarily for use by home-based raters such as parents. It may also be used by community-based informants such as supervisors and child care professionals. The HCSBS is a companion instrument to the SSBS-2, which is similar to the HCSBS but designed to be used by teachers or other school-based raters. Together, the HCSBS and SSBS-2 provide a comprehensive cross-informant system of screening and assessment for evaluating the social competence and antisocial behavior of children and youth. The HCSBS items, scales, and subscales were developed based on specific theories of social and antisocial behavior. Like all behavior rating scales, the HCSBS should be used within the constraints of its advantages and limitations. The remaining chapters of this manual provide specific instructions for administering, scoring, and interpreting the HCSBS (Chapters 2 and 3), as well as detailed information on the development, standardization, and technical properties of this instrument (Chapters 4, 5, and 6).

ADMINISTRATION AND SCORING PROCEDURES 2

This chapter provides instructions for completing the HCSBS rating form, information regarding user qualifications, and detailed directions for scoring the rating form.

COMPLETING THE RATING FORM

The HCSBS rating form was designed to be completed by parents of children and youth ages 5–18. It may also be completed by other family members, such as stepparents or grandparents, or a child's guardian or other caregivers. In addition, the rating form may be completed by adults who work with the child or adolescent in community settings, such as youth group leaders, group home staff, or supervisors. The primary criterion for determining if an individual is an appropriate rater is that he or she is knowledgeable about the child or adolescent's behavior in home and community settings. Teachers or other potential raters who are familiar with a child or youth in educational settings should rate the child or youth using the HCSBS's companion measure, the SSBS-2.

Completion of the rating form usually takes between 8 and 10 minutes. First, the *Identifying Information* section on page 1 should be completed as fully as possible. This section includes spaces to enter information regarding the child or adolescent (name, school, grade, age, gender) as well as information regarding the rater (name, relationship to child or adolescent, date completed, settings in which behavior is observed). This section should also be completed carefully so that individuals who use the results will have relevant information about the person who completed the rating form, as well as the correct demographic information about the child or adolescent for whom the rating form was completed.

After the rater has carefully read the instructions on page 1, he or she rates each item on the Social Competence (Scale A) and Antisocial Behavior (Scale B) scales, which are found on pages 2 and 3 of the rating form. Every item on each of the two scales must be rated, even if the rater is not exactly sure how to rate a specific item. If the rater is not sure how to complete a particular item, it should be estimated as accurately as possible. Items should not be left blank. Failure to rate all items makes interpretation of the results difficult and in some cases impossible. In most cases raters will complete all items as directed. Providing an additional verbal reminder to the rater to complete all of the items and glancing quickly at the rating form immediately after it has been completed are two simple strategies that will help to ensure that the rating form is completed in the correct manner. Note that the Social Competence and Antisocial Behavior scales on pages 2 and 3 of the rating form are labeled simply as "Scale A" and "Scale B," respectively. The names of the scales are not included on these sections of the rating form so that raters will not be influenced by the labels assigned to groups of rating items and will rate each item based solely on its content.

After all of the items have been completed, raters may provide additional information about the child or adolescent in the *Additional Information* section on the top of page 4. Although it is optional and not necessary for scoring the HCSBS, providing this information is recommended because it may provide important insight to those individuals who will interpret the scores.

When completed, the rating form should be given to the individual who is responsible for its scoring and interpretation.

Spanish Language HCSBS Rating Form

To assist in assessing children and adolescents whose parents or guardians speak primarily or exclusively Spanish, a Spanish language version of the HCSBS rating form is available. The Spanish language HCSBS rating form is completed the same way as the English version. The rating form is entirely in Spanish except for the HCSBS Score Summary section on page 4 of the form, which is in English. Raters are instructed (in Spanish) that the HCSBS Score Summary section of the form is for scorer use only.

USER QUALIFICATIONS

The HCSBS may be used by professionals from a variety of education and mental health fields. This section details the specific qualifications needed for various uses, including completing, scoring, and interpreting the rating form.

Qualifications for Completing the Rating Form

The only qualifications for rating a child or adolescent using the HCSBS rating form are that the rater should know the child or adolescent well enough to make an informed judgment of his or her behavior in home and community settings and that the rater should have the ability to read and comprehend either the English or Spanish version of the form and provide appropriate ratings and other information. In cases where an important potential rater cannot complete the HCSBS rating form because of reading or writing difficulties, it is permissible to have a trained interviewer read the rating form and items to the rater, elicit his or her responses, and complete the form for him or her. In the Directions section of page 1 of the rating form, raters are given the following instruction: *Ratings should be based on your observations of this child or adolescent's behavior* **during the past three months** (italics added for emphasis). Therefore, individuals other than the child or adolescent's parents should have had the opportunity to observe and interact with the child for a minimum of 3 months before rating the child using the HCSBS.

Qualifications for Scoring the Rating Form

Scoring the HCSBS rating form is straightforward. No special expertise or computer software is required. All one needs to do is read the manual carefully and practice. In most cases, scoring will be done by the same person who is responsible for interpreting the scores. A properly trained clerical worker may also score the rating form.

Qualifications for Interpreting the Results

Individuals who interpret the HCSBS results should have a basic understanding of the principles of educational and psychological testing, including the standards for testing that have been developed jointly by the American Educational Research Association, American Psychological Association, and National Council on Measurement in Education (AERA, APA, & NCME, 1999). Because the HCSBS is a screening instrument designed for use across a wide variety of settings, and because interpretation procedures are straightforward and clearly defined in this manual, these individuals need not be licensed psychologists. Other trained professionals such as social workers, counselors, speech-language pathologists, educational diagnosticians, and teachers who have received appropriate training in educational and psychological measurement may also interpret the results.

Specific training in understanding and assessing the behavior and emotional problems of children and youth is also recommended for optimal use of the HCSBS. This manual contains specific information regarding the psychometric properties of the HCSBS. This information may be very helpful in understanding and correctly using the test; however, the *ultimate responsibility for correct and appropriate use of the HCSBS rests with the user. This instrument should be used only for purposes described in this manual.*

Individuals who use HCSBS data to assist in developing individualized education programs (IEPs), positive behavior support plans, or other types of interventions should have a sound understanding of normal and abnormal social and behavioral development of children and adolescents. Knowledge of specific behavioral, cognitive, and affective intervention techniques is especially important when developing interventions for children and youth. Chapter 3 provides additional details on recommendations for linking assessment results to intervention.

DIRECTIONS FOR SCORING THE RATING FORM

Scoring the HCSBS rating form involves four simple steps:

1. Calculate raw scores for the two Social Competence subscales and the two Antisocial Behavior subscales.
2. Calculate total raw scores for the Social Competence and Antisocial Behavior scales.
3. Convert raw scores to *T*-scores and percentile ranks.
4. Identify and record Social Functioning Levels (SFLs) corresponding to subscale and total raw scores.

These steps are described in detail in this section.

Step 1: Calculate Subscale Raw Scores

Raw scores for the HCSBS subscales are calculated by entering the circled value for each item into the nonshaded scoring key column with which it corresponds on page 2 or 3 of the rating form and then summing the values entered for each of the vertical columns. The vertical columns represent the HCSBS subscales.

There are two vertical subscale columns for the Social Competence scale (Scale A): Peer Relations (labeled PR) and Self-Management/Compliance (labeled SMC). The Antisocial Behavior scale (Scale B) also has two of these vertical columns to reflect two subscales: Defiant/Disruptive (DD) and Antisocial/Aggressive (AA). The sums of each vertical column are entered at the bottom of the scoring key, in the blank boxes located to the right of the word *Totals*, just above the subscale abbreviations. These subscale raw scores are then entered into the Raw Score section of the *HCSBS Score Summary* table on page 4 of the rating form.

Dealing with Missing Data   From time to time, a rater may leave one or more items blank. The following procedures are recommended in such cases.

- If three or fewer items for either of the two major scales are not rated, scorers should enter values for those items by determining the most common or modal rated value for ratings of other items within that scale.

    For example, if two items in the Social Competence scale are not completed, the scorer should glance at values circled for the other 30 items in that scale, determine which value (1, 2, 3, 4, or 5) has been circled most frequently, and enter this value in the scoring key for the two missing items. This procedure will allow HCSBS users to score and interpret the rating form without compromising the psychometric integrity of the results.

- If four or more items in either of the two major scales have not been completed, do not score the rating form.

In such cases the rating form may be completed by contacting the rater and helping him or her complete the missing items. If such efforts are unsuccessful, the items on the rating form should only be viewed informally to glean some general impressions regarding the rater's perceptions about the child's behavioral adjustment. To repeat, the *rating form is not scored when four or more items within a scale are not rated.*

Step 2: Calculate Total Raw Scores

Total raw scores for the Social Competence and Antisocial Behavior scales are simply a sum of the raw scores of the subscales within each scale. There are no cross-loading items on either scale. To calculate the Social Competence Total raw score, add the raw score values for the Peer Relations and Self-Management/Compliance subscales that have been entered in the corresponding Raw Score boxes on the HCSBS Score Summary table on page 4 of the rating form, and enter the sum of these two raw scores in the Raw Score box that corresponds to Social Competence Total. To calculate the Antisocial Behavior Total raw score, add the raw score values for the Defiant/Disruptive and Antisocial/Aggressive subscales that have been entered in the corresponding Raw Score boxes on the HCSBS Score Summary table on page 4 of the rating form, and then enter the sum of these two raw scores in the Raw Score box that corresponds to Antisocial Behavior Total.

Step 3: Convert Raw Scores to *T*-Scores and Percentile Ranks

After the subscale and total raw scores have been calculated and entered in the appropriate boxes in the HCSBS Score Summary table on page 4 of the rating form, they are converted to *T*-scores and percentile ranks. These values are then entered into the corresponding box in the HCSBS Score Summary table. The raw score conversions are made by referring to the tables in Appendix A for scores of children ages 5–11 and by referring to the tables in Appendix B for scores of youth ages 12–18.

The process of converting raw scores to *T*-scores and percentile ranks is simple. The scorer identifies the appropriate raw score for a given subscale or total score in the appropriate table and then determines which *T*-score and percentile rank correspond horizontally to the raw scores. These corresponding values are then entered in the appropriate box in the HCSBS Score Summary table on page 4 of the rating form.

Step 4: Identify and Record Social Functioning Levels

SFLs corresponding to HCSBS scores are also simple to identify. Refer to the charts labeled *Social Functioning Levels* at the bottom of each table in Appendix A and Appendix B to determine the correct SFL corresponding to specific raw score ranges for each subscale and total score from that table, and then enter these SFLs in the appropriate box in the HCSBS Score Summary table on page 4 of the rating form. For ease of identification, the SFLs for the Social Competence scale and Antisocial Behavior scale are divided from each other by a dark horizontal line. For the Social Competence scale, there are four SFLs: *High Functioning, Average, At-Risk,* and *High Risk.* For the Antisocial Behavior Scale, there are three SFLs: *Average, At-Risk,* and *High Risk.* More details on the SFLs are provided in Chapter 3.

SUMMARY

The rating form is simple to complete and to score. Children and youth may be rated by parents or other home- and community-based adults who are knowledgeable regarding their behavior. No special expertise or computer programs are required to score the rating form. This chapter describes the basic rating and scoring procedures and identifies the tables in Appendix A and Appendix B that are consulted in the scoring process. The quick reference guide lists the four steps for scoring the HCSBS rating form.

Quick Reference: Steps for scoring the HCSBS rating form

1. Calculate subscale raw scores.

2. Calculate total raw scores.

3. Convert raw scores to *T*-scores and percentile ranks (use tables in Appendix A for ages 5–11; use tables in Appendix B for ages 12–18).

4. Identify and record Social Functioning Levels (SFLs) corresponding to subscale and total raw scores (SFLs are located in Appendix A and Appendix B).

INTERPRETING AND USING HCSBS SCORES   3

After the HCSBS rating form has been completed and scored, the results may be used to help better understand observed patterns of social and antisocial behavior of children and youth who have been rated using this instrument. Results may also be useful in assisting clinicians in making decisions regarding educational program placement, diagnostic classification, and intervention planning.

A three-level approach to interpreting HCSBS scores is suggested. The first level involves interpreting the *T*-scores and percentile ranks as indicators of score placement. The second level involves interpreting the SFLs. The third level involves qualitative inspection of individual items. Each of these three levels of score interpretation is described in this chapter. Some additional information that may be helpful in interpreting scores is also provided, namely information regarding cross-informant assessment with the HCSBS and SSBS-2, using the HCSBS in functional behavioral assessment (FBA), and linking assessment information to intervention planning.

THREE-LEVEL INTERPRETATION STRATEGY

This section describes the suggested three-level interpretation strategy in detail. Two case studies are described in the following section to provide examples of how each of the three interpretation levels might be applied.

Interpretation Level 1: *T*-Scores and Percentile Ranks

The first level of interpretation involves examining scores in terms of where they are in relation to other scores from the appropriate HCSBS norming sample, namely *T*-scores and percentile ranks. The information yielded from this level of interpretation is useful in making comparative judgments regarding where a child or youth's HCSBS scores are in relation to those scores of other individuals in the norming sample.

T-Scores   The subscale and total raw scores are converted to *T*-scores using the appropriate score conversion tables in Appendix A (for children ages 5–11) or Appendix B (for youth ages 12–18). These *T*-scores were developed using a linear transformation of raw scores and are based on a mean of 50 and standard deviation of 10. *T*-scores are generally familiar to educators and mental health professionals who routinely use behavior rating scales and personality tests. Many well-known behavior and personality measures for children and youth use a *T*-score system for converting raw scores.

The general interpretation structure of *T*-scores is that a score of 50 indicates placement at the mean or average level of the norm sample. Given that the standard deviation is set at 10, a *T*-score of 60 would thus indicate that the score is approximately 1 standard deviation higher than the mean of the norming sample. A *T*-score of 40 would be approximately 1 standard deviation below the normative mean.

In evaluating HCSBS *T*-scores, you should consider two basic issues regarding their meaning. First, as is indicated below the HCSBS Score Summary table on page 4 of the rating form, *higher Social Competence scores always indicate greater levels of social adjustment, and higher Antisocial Behavior scores always indicate greater levels of social behavior problems.* Therefore, high scores on the Social Competence scale should be viewed as desirable or good, and low scores on this scale should be viewed as problematic and indicating deficits in social competence. Conversely, high scores on the Antisocial Behavior scale may be cause for concern, whereas low scores are desirable because they indicate fewer problems.

The second issue you should consider in interpreting *T*-scores is that *scores from the HCSBS norming samples do not exactly follow the pattern of a "bell shaped" curve.* Rather, *both the Social Competence and Antisocial Behavior score distributions are somewhat skewed in the direction of more ratings indicating desirable behavior and fewer scores indicating undesirable behavior.* This distribution is simply a reflection of the way that typical norm samples for child behavior ratings appear (see Merrell, 2000a and 2000b for discussions of normal distributions in child behavior rating scale scores). More children have adequate or good social-behavioral adjustment than have social-behavioral deficits or problems. This situation is not unique to the HCSBS; all child and adolescent behavior rating scales share this measurement phenomenon because the constructs that they measure are not normally distributed. Some test developers choose to "smooth" or normalize score distributions to make them conform to a normal bell-shaped curve such as would be found with the score distributions of educational achievement or cognitive ability test scores, for the purpose of making scores easier for some users to interpret. This smoothing or normalization approach was rejected for the HCSBS and SSBS-2 because it is arbitrary and does not reflect accurately the natural shape of behavior score distributions. There is no sound theoretical basis for making such arbitrary "smoothing" decisions for child behavior rating scale scores.

Because the HCSBS *T*-score distributions retain their naturally occurring shape, you should recognize that the standard deviation units based on a value of 10 may only be close approximations, particularly as individual scores move farther away from the normative mean for that score. In other words, a standard score of 70 may not always reflect that the particular score in question is *exactly* 2 standard deviations higher than the normative mean of 50, although it should be very close to this level.

Percentile Ranks A percentile rank or percentile score expresses the percentage of cases in the HCSBS norming samples that fall below a specific score. Percentiles may be viewed as ranks in a group of 100 representative cases or subjects, with 1 being the lowest rank and 100 the highest. Thus, a percentile score of 79 would indicate that the particular score in question was equal to or higher than 79% of the cases or subjects in the sample. In addition, a percentile score of 79 would indicate that the score is in the highest 21% of scores for the sample. Again, for appropriate interpretation, it is important to remember the directionality of HCSBS scores, including percentile scores. If a child or adolescent's obtained HCSBS Social Competence Total score was at the 95th percentile, that score would be interpreted as being in the highest 5% of social skills scores for that distribution, something that should be valued highly. On the other hand, if an Antisocial Behavior Total score was at the 95th percentile, that score would indicate that this child or adolescent's observed levels of antisocial problem behavior were equal to or higher than 95% of the norming sample, or in the highest 5%. A score at this level for the Problem Behavior scale would certainly raise concern about the child's social-behavioral adjustment and the possible need for intervention services.

Interpretation Level 2: Social Functioning Levels

The second suggested level of interpretation for HCSBS scores involves the use of SFLs to understand the relative meaning of the child or adolescent's scores on each scale and subscale. These SFLs were developed to indicate the general level of social-behavioral adjustment indicated by the HCSBS scores. Four SFLs are utilized for the Social Competence scores, and three SFLs are used with the Antisocial Behavior scores. The meaning and interpretation of these SFLs are discussed by scale in this section. The SFLs for the HCSBS are based in general on the same rationale as the popular prevention-oriented "tiered" approach to behavior and instructional support that is often presented as a three-tier or four-tier triangle (see Merrell, Ervin, & Gimpel, 2006, as well as the web site for the National Technical Assistance Center for Positive Behavioral Interventions and Supports at http://www.pbis.org for more details on the tiered approach to prevention). The meaning and interpretation of these SFLs are discussed by scale in this section.

Social Competence Scale: Four Social Functioning Levels For scores on the Social Competence scale (Scale A), there are four SFLs: *High Functioning, Average, At-Risk,* and *High Risk*. Each of these SFLs indicates Social Competence scores within differing functional ranges of the normative distribution.

The *High Functioning* level includes raw scores that are above 80% of the norm group scores for the Social Competence subscale or total scores. Scores at this level reflect ratings of excellent social competence. Children and adolescents whose total score or more than one subscale score are at this level are likely to have excellent relationships with peers, teachers, and others. They are typically viewed as being socially skilled, outgoing, well-adjusted, and personable.

The *Average* level includes Social Competence scores that range from approximately the 80th to the 20th percentile levels of the norm group. Children or youth who exhibit typical, adequate, or nonremarkable levels of social competence will likely receive scores in this range. The majority of cases in the norming samples (about 60%) have Social Competence scores at this level.

The *At-Risk* level includes scores that range from approximately the 20th to the 5th percentile ranks of the norm group for Social Competence scores. Children and adolescents who are rated as having Social Competence scores at this level are close to or slightly more than 1 standard deviation below the normative mean. They are good candidates for more comprehensive assessment of their social behavior. With further evaluation, a clinician can determine whether students whose Social Competence scores are in this range might benefit from a social-emotional learning intervention or some other type of attention.

The *High Risk* level includes scores similar to approximately 5% of the norm group with the lowest Social Competence scores (below the 5th percentile rank). Children and adolescents whose HCSBS ratings are in this range are likely to have significant acquisition or performance deficits in their social skills, poor peer relationships, and poor social competence in general. If a student receives a Social Competence Total score or one or more Social Competence subscale scores at the *High Risk* level, he or she should be evaluated in more detail. It is very likely that the child or adolescent's social competence deficits and peer adjustment problems are so substantial that he or she is experiencing significant adjustment problems and that the child or adolescent would benefit from a carefully designed social skills training or interpersonal skills intervention. The most problematic 5% was selected for inclusion in the *High Risk* level based on prevalence estimates that indicate that approximately 3%–6% of the school-age population exhibit social skills deficits to a great enough extent that special education or other specific social-emotional interventions are desirable for treatment of existing deficits and to prevent the occurrence of more serious social behavior problems (Cullinan, Epstein, & Kauffman, 1984; Kauffman, 2000; Merrell, 2008; Merrell & Gimpel, 1998).

Antisocial Behavior Scale: Three Social Functioning Levels Unlike the Social Competence scale, which includes four SFLs, the Antisocial Behavior scale (Scale B) includes three SFLs: *Average, At-Risk,* and *High Risk.* There are two reasons for the differing number of SFLs across the two scales. First, the score distributions on the Antisocial Behavior scale are more skewed than distributions of Social Competence scores, with a large percentage of student ratings evidencing little or no problem behavior. Thus, making a distinction between average and high functioning students in this regard would be very arbitrary. Second, whereas the construct of social competence lends itself to a natural distinction between average functioning and high functioning, the construct of antisocial behavior does not. With regard to engagement in antisocial behavior, it is difficult to say that one level of behavior would make one "high functioning," whereas another level would make one "average." The absence of problem behavior does not necessarily indicate that a child or adolescent is high functioning with respect to his or her social-behavioral adjustment.

The *Average* level includes Antisocial Behavior scores that are lower than those received by 80% of the appropriate norm group, or in other words, below the 80th percentile rank. Students who receive Antisocial Behavior scores at this level are likely to exhibit few or no antisocial behavior problems of concern and are not likely to require any additional screening or attention in this area.

The *At-Risk* level for Antisocial Behavior reflects scores that range from approximately the 80th to the 95th percentile ranks in comparison with similar age peers. Students who receive an Antisocial Behavior Total score or more than one Antisocial Behavior subscale score at the At-Risk level should be carefully evaluated because of the possibility that they may be developing a pattern of antisocial behavior that might require some prevention efforts. Not all students who receive scores in the At-Risk level will require such prevention efforts, but it would be wise to at least consider their social-behavioral functioning in more detail.

The *High Risk* level for Antisocial Behavior includes scores in the highest 5% of the normative group frequency distribution, or in other words, at approximately the 96th percentile rank and higher. Thus, the High Risk level reflects teacher ratings of significant antisocial behavior problems. Students who have a Social Competence Total score or more than one Social Competence subscale score at the High Risk level are very likely to be exhibiting significant antisocial behavior problems. It is likely that this level of problems will cause significant adjustment problems in the school environment. It is also likely that students whose antisocial behavior problems are at this level are at very high risk for having or developing conduct disorders or various types of delinquent behavior. Students whose Antisocial Behavior scores are at this level should *definitely* be evaluated in more depth for the possibility of providing specially designed educational programming and prevention or intervention programs to help reduce their antisocial behavior problems and prevent the onset of more serious problems. Like the High Risk level for the Social Competence scale, the most problematic 5% of Antisocial Behavior scores were selected as the cutoff point for this level because of various prevalence estimates indicating that approximately this percentage of the school-age population exhibits antisocial behavior problems to a great enough extent that special education or other specific behavioral interventions are desirable (Cullinan, Epstein, & Kauffman, 1984; Kauffman, 2000; Merrell, 2008; Merrell & Gimpel, 1998).

Interpretation Level 3:
Qualitative Inspection of Individual Items

When any of the HCSBS scores are in the At-Risk or High Risk ranges, it is advisable to conduct a qualitative inspection of the ratings of individual items. The major purpose of item-level inspection is to identify specific behavioral concerns. If particular items of concern are noted, look for commonalities among the identified items, determine whether a trend in deficits or problems appears to be present, and generate hypotheses regarding potential intervention strategies and targets. Alternatively, individual items, particularly the items on the Social Competence scale, may be evaluated to identify strengths of a given child or youth. In either case, individual items of the HCSBS may be helpful in developing goal statements or targets for intervention.

Evaluating Social Competence Items *When any scores from the Social Competence scale are at the At-Risk or High Risk levels, individual items within that scale that have received ratings of 1 or 2 should be examined further.* A rating of 1 or 2 on an item of the Social Competence scale indicates that the rater perceived that the target child or youth exhibits that particular desirable behavior or characteristic never or almost never. The first issue in evaluating individual Social Competence items rated at this level is to consider whether some of them are functionally more important than others. It may be that rarely engaging in some social skills is not much of a problem, whereas rarely engaging in other social skills may be creating social problems that lead to peer rejection. The second question to consider is whether the Social Competence items that are targeted deficits cluster together in any meaningful way. It may be that patterns of items where there are noteworthy deficits may reveal specific patterns of concern and may be useful in generating hypotheses regarding the characteristics of the problem and how to best develop an intervention plan to increase positive social behaviors.

Evaluating Antisocial Behavior Items *When any scores from the Antisocial Behavior scale are at the At-Risk or High Risk levels, individual items within that scale that have received ratings of 4 or 5 should be examined further.* A rating of 4 or 5 on an item of the Antisocial Behavior scale indicates that the rater perceived that the target child or youth exhibits that particular problem behavior or characteristic frequently, or to a greater-than-average level. The first question to consider in evaluating individual Antisocial Behavior items in this manner is to determine if any of the identified problem areas are of more functional importance than others or are more of an obstacle to the child or youth achieving positive social adjustment. The second question to consider is whether the Antisocial Behavior items that are rated as being a concern cluster together in any meaningful way. It may be that patterns of problem items where there are noteworthy excesses may reveal specific clusters or types of concern. This procedure may be useful in generating hypotheses regarding the topography of the problem and how to best develop an intervention plan to decrease antisocial behaviors and increase positive social behaviors that are incompatible with those problems.

CASE STUDIES

To aid users of the HCSBS in interpreting scores according to the three-level interpretation strategy recommended in this chapter, two case studies are presented to illustrate how to proceed through the interpretation process. These case studies use fictitious names and identifying information but are based on actual cases and score patterns from the national norming sample.

Case Study 1: Jeff

Jeff is a 17-year-old boy who was rated on the HCSBS by his father. He attends a public high school, where he is in the 11th grade. Jeff's scores and SFLs are presented in Table 3.1.

For the Social Competence scale, his *T*-scores range from 41 to 47, and his percentile ranks range from 21 to 34. Jeff's father rated Jeff's positive social behavior at a level that would be considered to be average or typical. His Social Competence subscale scores and total score are all within 1 standard deviation of the norming sample mean for ages 12–18. All three of Jeff's Social Competence scores are at the Average level, so it is not necessary to examine his individual Social Competence scale item scores. It is worthwhile noting, however, that Jeff's father did rate 4 of the 32 Social Competence items with a value of 5, indicating that these areas are perceived as strengths for Jeff. These items include *Has skills or abilities that are admired by peers* (Item 11), *Interacts with a wide variety of peers* (Item 19), *Is good at initiating or joining conversations with peers* (Item 21), and *Has good leadership skills* (Item 26). Although Jeff's score on the Peer Relations subscale is in the Average range rather than the High Functioning range, it is interesting to note that the five items where his father noted him to have specific strengths are all on the Peer Relations subscale.

With respect to his Antisocial Behavior scores, Jeff's *T*-scores range from 55 to 73, and his percentile ranks range from 75 to 97. These scores show

Table 3.1. HCSBS Scores for Jeff (case study 1)

HCSBS scale	Raw score	*T*-score	Percentile rank	SFL
Peer Relations	64	47	34	Average
Self-Management/Compliance	47	41	21	Average
Social Competence Total	111	44	25	Average
Defiant/Disruptive	35	55	75	Average
Antisocial/Aggressive	51	73	97	High Risk
Antisocial Behavior Total	86	64	90	At-Risk

Key: SFL, Social Functioning Level.

some complexity and concern in the problem behavior ratings provided by Jeff's father. His Antisocial/Aggressive subscale score and his Antisocial Behavior Total score are both more than 1 standard deviation higher than the normative mean. Although the Defiant/ Disruptive subscale score is at the Average level, his Antisocial/ Aggressive and Antisocial Behavior Total scores are at the High Risk and At-Risk levels, respectively. Therefore, it is clear that Jeff's rated level of antisocial behavior should be a cause for additional evaluation and examination.

Jeff's father rated five of the individual items on the Antisocial Behavior scale with a value of 4, indicating that he perceives these behaviors as occurring at a relatively frequent rate. These individual items include *Gets into fights* (Item 5), *Teases and makes fun of others* (Item 7), *Threatens others; is verbally aggressive* (Item 17), *Swears or uses offensive language* (Item 18), and *Boasts and brags* (Item 27). These five items indicate perceptions of a propensity for some conflict with peers at times as well as some mild violation of social norms. These particular characteristics, however, are not necessarily indicative of the types of severe antisocial behavior that might lead to gang activity, delinquency, or involvement with the juvenile justice system. Some follow-up regarding *Gets into fights* and *Threatens others; is verbally aggressive* might be useful. Although Jeff's father indicated that Jeff engages in these behaviors on a relatively frequent basis, we know nothing about the specific ways in which Jeff engages in them and how serious they are.

In the Additional Information section on page 4 of the rating form, Jeff's father wrote the following comments: "Jeff gets along very well with other kids a lot of the time, and he has a few very good friends. But he can come across as pushy or threatening to other kids sometimes. Some of them won't hang out with him because they are mad at him. At home he is a great kid most of the time, although he is kind of a slacker who would rather play or party than do about anything else. He is loving, fun, and can always make me laugh."

Overall Jeff's results from his father's rating portray a young man who has adequate to good social competence, particularly in the peer-related social-adjustment domain. Jeff, however, is also seen as engaging in certain antisocial behaviors to a troublesome level. These results present somewhat of a paradox. On one hand, Jeff is rated as having overall adequate to good peer relationships and some excellent peer-relations skills, but he is also seen as exhibiting some antisocial behaviors to a troubling level, including fighting and making threats. This seeming paradox is illustrated by some of the anecdotal comments that Jeff's father provided in the Additional Information section, where he indicated that Jeff has many positive qualities, is fun to be around, and has several friends but also alienates or distances peers.

Jeff's profile of scores is quite reminiscent of what Coie et al. (1982) termed *controversial* youth. Youth who fit the profile of being controversial are perceived as being assertive and somewhat likeable leaders who alienate peers and act in coercive ways at times. Based on these assessment data alone, it is unclear whether any interventions are warranted; however, additional assessment would certainly be helpful to clarify some of the concerns.

Obtaining social behavior ratings from other sources and settings (school, teachers) would be useful, as would behavioral interviewing with Jeff, his father, and teachers regarding the intensity, target, and problem level of his problem behaviors. Consistent with the FBA approach, if it is deemed that Jeff's level of antisocial behavior is truly a significant problem, it would also be useful to pinpoint the most problematic behaviors and generate hypotheses regarding what is promoting or maintaining these behaviors.

Case Study 2: Carrie

Carrie is a 9-year-old girl who is in the third grade. Carrie's mother completed the HCSBS rating form. A summary of Carrie's scores and SFLs is presented in Table 3.2.

For the Social Competence scale, Carrie received *T*-scores ranging from 20 to 40 and percentile ranks ranging from 1 to 17. These scores are all indicative of moderate to significant deficits in social competence and range from 1 to 3 standard deviations below the normative mean. Her Peer Relations and Social Competence Total scores are at the High Risk level, whereas her Self-Management/Compliance score is at the At-Risk level. Overall, Carrie's Social Competence scores indicate substantial deficits in adaptive social skills and other positive social behaviors, especially in the peer-related domain of social adjustment.

Qualitative inspection of individual items from the Social Competence scale that Carrie's mother assigned values of 1 or 2 reveals a large number of positive social characteristics where Carrie's mother rated her quite low. Of the 32 items in this scale, 9 were assigned values of 1, and 9 were assigned values of 2.

Carrie's mother rated the following items with values of 1, indicating Never:

- Remains calm when problems arise (Item 7)
- Has skills or abilities that are admired by peers (Item 11)
- Interacts with a wide variety of peers (Item 19)
- Is good at initiating or joining conversations with peers (Item 21)

Table 3.2. HCSBS scores for Carrie (case study 2)

HCSBS scale	Raw score	*T*-score	Percentile rank	SFL
Peer Relations	27	20	1	High Risk
Self-Management/Compliance	43	40	17	At-Risk
Social Competence Total	70	28	3	High Risk
Defiant/Disruptive	28	47	45	Average
Antisocial/Aggressive	22	45	43	Average
Antisocial Behavior Total	50	46	43	Average

Key: SFL, Social Functioning Level.

- Enters appropriately into ongoing activities with peers (Item 25)
- Has good leadership skills (Item 26)
- Notices and compliments accomplishments of others (Item 28)
- Is invited by peers to join in activities (Item 30)
- Is "looked up to" or respected by peers (Item 32)

Carrie's mother rated the following items with values of 2, a mid-point between Sometimes and Never that indicates a low rate of occurrence:

- Cooperates with peers (Item 1)
- Offers help to peers when needed (Item 4)
- Understands problems and needs of peers (Item 6)
- Invites peers to participate in activities (Item 9)
- Is accepting of peers (Item 12)
- Will give in or compromise with peers when appropriate (Item 15)
- Is sensitive to the feelings of others (Item 22)
- Controls temper when angry (Item 24)
- Is assertive in an appropriate way when he or she needs to be (Item 29)

In contrast to her Social Competence scores, Carrie's scores on the Antisocial Behavior scale are all within normal limits and are generally unremarkable. Her *T*-scores range from 45 to 47, and her percentile ranks range from 43 to 45. The three Antisocial Behavior scores are all at the Average level, and none of the individual items on this scale were rated higher than 3 (indicating Sometimes).

Carrie's mother wrote the following comments in the Additional Information section on page 4 of the rating form: "Carrie is very shy. She would like to have friends but the other kids are often cruel to her—they don't understand her, make fun of her, and leave her out of things they do. When she does things to try and make friends, she usually gets hurt. She is very good to me and she loves animals. I try and protect her from being hurt but I can only do so much."

Overall, Carrie's pattern of scores and item ratings from the HCSBS completed by her mother portray a girl who is seriously deficient in adaptive social behavior characteristics, particularly in areas related to forming positive relationships with peers. Although Carrie is not rated as exhibiting an unusual rate of problem behaviors, her significant deficits in social skills and the accompanying peer relationship problems undoubtedly put her at very high risk for negative outcomes. Assuming that the pattern of social behavior ratings provided by Carrie's mother is consistent across settings, it evidences a combination of being simultaneously socially neglected and socially rejected by peers and is probably fueled in great measure by Carrie's poorly developed social skills. The narrative comments provided by Carrie's mother in the Additional Materials section are revealing. She noted that Carrie is shy and that Carrie would like to have friends but is misunderstood, excluded, and teased by her peers.

In terms of a suggested plan of follow-up from Carrie's HCSBS scores, it seems very important to obtain cross-informant ratings of her social behavior from one or more teachers at school using the SSBS-2. The addition of school-based ratings to Carrie's HCSBS scores would help to verify whether the serious social competence deficits noted by Carrie's mother are perceived as existing across settings. If these deficits do appear to be stable across settings, then intervention is clearly warranted. Social skills training that specifically targets the domain of peer relationship behaviors appears to be the most immediate target for intervention. In addition, some additional screening might be useful to evaluate Carrie's emotional status. It is easy to hypothesize that Carrie may be experiencing high levels of depression and anxiety symptoms and, because the HCSBS does not target the internalizing domain of problem behavior, it may be useful to conduct follow-up assessment with interviews and child self-report instruments to ascertain Carrie's level of adjustment in this area. It is likely that an effective intervention for Carrie will need to involve more than just simple social skills training.

CROSS-INFORMANT ASSESSMENT WITH THE HCSBS

It is important to remember that the HCSBS was designed for a variety of purposes and that one of the most important purposes is to serve as one component of a comprehensive assessment design. When used in this manner, information from the HCSBS may be useful in making diagnostic and classification decisions, determining program eligibility, and so forth. No single instrument, including the HCSBS or SSBS-2, should be used as the sole basis for making these types of decisions.

There are certain situations, such as routine screening, where a single behavior rating scale completed by one rater is sufficient; however, for most other purposes, the tenets of the multimethod, multisource, multisetting assessment design that are discussed in Chapter 1 should be followed to the greatest extent that the circumstances will allow. The particular application of this principle for use with behavior rating scales is usually referred to as *cross-informant assessment* because behavior ratings using the same instrument or similar instruments are obtained across differing informants, each of whom will have their own unique set of experiences and observations on which to base their ratings.

If home-based informants are the sole possible source of information, it is recommended that at least two different raters (e.g., mother and father, mother and grandparent) rate the child or adolescent using the HCSBS. In situations beyond routine screening where the circumstances allow, it is strongly recommended that home-based ratings on the HCSBS be consolidated with school-based ratings from its companion measure, the SSBS-2. Again, it is recommended that in such instances the premise of cross-informant assessment be followed to the greatest extent possible. Ideally, HCSBS ratings from more than one home-based rater will be consolidated with SSBS-2 ratings from more than one school-based rater. The resulting assessment data will provide an aggregated portrait of the child or adolescent's social behavior from multiple sources, across settings, and across instruments.

Although aggregated behavior ratings are the recommended practice, it is often challenging to effectively consolidate and interpret behavior ratings obtained from multiple sources, and if one is not careful, error variance may actually be increased (see Merrell, 2008, for more details). Consider the following suggestions as ways of assisting in the process of data aggregation:

- Be less concerned about the actual score levels (T-scores, percentile ranks, SFLs) on ratings from differing sources and more concerned about commonalities in trends and patterns.

- Look for patterns of social-behavioral strengths, deficits, and problems that are indicated by more than one rater and across more than one setting. If similar general trends are observed, there is a high probability that the particular pattern of observed social behavior is consistent or stable.

- In situations where significant social-behavioral deficits or problems are evident from more than one rater and across settings, try to isolate the critical common clusters of behavior by developing a matrix of subscale scores where At-Risk or High Risk levels are indicated.

- In situations where many problems or deficits are indicated across raters and settings but the pattern is diffuse, try to identify the critical common ratings by conducting a qualitative item analysis. Start by listing the items where at least one rater has assigned a value of 1 (for Social Competence items) or 5 (for Antisocial Behavior items), and then note how many raters assigned a similar rating to that item. If it seems useful, expand the range of assigned values to 1 and 2 for the Social Competence items and 4 and 5 for the Antisocial Behavior items.

Although interpretation of aggregated social behavior ratings from multiple sources and across settings may be challenging, this method is the preferred option whenever possible. Using the HCSBS and SSBS-2 in a cross-informant design will help to overcome the limitations of any one source of information or the situational specificity of any one setting in which the child or adolescent's behavior is observed.

USING THE HCSBS IN FUNCTIONAL BEHAVIORAL ASSESSMENT

Since the mid-1990s, FBA procedures have been increasingly used to identify behavior, social, emotional, and academic problems in children and youth and to help link these problems to effective interventions. This interest has been most apparent in the fields of special education and school psychology because of federally mandated requirements for assessment practice with students who have behavior and emotional problems. These requirements were included in the Individuals with Disabilities Education Act Amendments of 1997 (PL 105-17). Although FBA procedures were originally developed as a tool for linking assessment to intervention for individuals with severe disabilities, the applications of FBA are quite broad.

The basis for FBA is relatively straightforward. It is a way of assessing behaviors to identify the particular *functions* of these behaviors. In other words, problem behaviors are assumed to serve a purpose in the child's environment, and these purposes sometimes maintain problems. For example, a child may engage in antisocial problem behaviors and may be reinforced for doing so because these behaviors allow him or her to escape unpleasant task demands or because they provide reinforcing social attention from peers or teachers. When using FBA, one seeks to determine relationships between the problem behaviors, *antecedents* that may elicit or bring forth the problems, and *consequences* of the behavior that may be maintaining it. *The goal of FBA is to develop hypotheses about probable functions that the problem behaviors may serve and to test these hypotheses by implementing an intervention.*

The HCSBS may be a useful tool in the initial process of developing and implementing an FBA. The most appropriate role for the HCSBS in this regard is to provide indirect information about a child or youth's social-behavioral competencies, deficits, and problems and to use the assessment results to generate initial hypotheses regarding the possible functions of these behaviors; however, behavior rating scales alone are insufficient for conducting a comprehensive functional assessment of behavior. The use of additional assessment methods, particularly direct behavioral observation and behavioral interviews with parents and teachers, are especially important in this process (Chafouleas, Riley-Tilman, & Sugai, 2007; Merrell, 2008).

FBA requires specific knowledge of applied behavior analysis as well as experience in assessing child behavior problems. Although the HCSBS may be used in the initial stages of conducting an FBA, a complete description of FBA is well beyond the scope of this manual. For a basic description of FBA and how to implement it, readers are referred to the following references: Crone and Horner (2003); Horner and Carr (1997); McComas, Hoch, and Mace (2000); and Watson and Steege (2003). Other sources of information are also available, but these four references are a solid starting point.

LINKING ASSESSMENT TO INTERVENTION

Although HCSBS scores can be useful in developing intervention plans at a general level by assisting in determining whether a social-behavioral intervention may be warranted, they can also play an important intervention design role at a more specific level. This role can be accomplished by looking at the overall profile of HCSBS scores and determining whether the child or adolescent has social deficits or behavior excesses in specific areas based on his or her subscale scores and then designing the intervention to focus on the areas of greatest concern. For example, in case study 2, Carrie's scores on the HCSBS Social Competence scale were problematic in general and indicated significant deficits in social skills; however, it was also evident from extremely low scores on the Peer Relations subscale (which resulted in assignment to the High Risk level) that her most serious social behavior problems involve difficulty in relating to peers appropriately and that she is at great risk for experiencing social rejection from peers. Such a behavioral profile indicates that the desired behavioral intervention should focus heavily on training for appropriate peer-relationship skills.

In many ways, a problem-specific or situation-specific approach to developing interventions is preferable to a global treatment approach that does not match the intervention to the problem. In fact, a review of recommended practices in working with children and youth with emotional or behavior disorders that was conducted by the Peacock Hill Working Group (1991) of the Council for Children with Behavioral Disorders emphasized that successful strategies address the specific problems of the child or youth at the level required by the severity of the problem. Thus, in using the HCSBS to develop appropriate intervention plans, specific areas of concern should be addressed, as well as global deficits. As in all cases, linking the assessment of an appropriate intervention will be accomplished most effectively if the assessment is multimethod in nature and does not rely solely on HCSBS scores or any other single instrument.

Another way that the HCSBS can be utilized in intervention planning is through examination of individual items. In the two case studies presented in this chapter, the process of examining specific items of concern and then using them in generating hypotheses and establishing intervention targets was illustrated. Individual HCSBS items can also be used to assist professionals and parents in the development of IEP goal statements for students who are receiving special education services. The items on the Social Competence scale can be incorporated directly into IEP goal statements because these items are worded positively. For example, if inspection of the HCSBS rating form for a particular child or adolescent reveals that he or she is consistently rated as Never on Item 2, *Makes appropriate transitions between different activities,* the IEP goal statement for a hypothetical student named Marcus might read "Marcus will make appropriate transitions between classroom activities," followed by the description of an appropriate percentage and observation method. For the items in the Antisocial Behavior scale, the wording can be rephrased slightly to reflect appropriate goal statements. For example, if a hypothetical student named Sandra consistently is rated at a high level (4 or 5) on Item 13, *Will not share with others,* the IEP goal statement might read "Sandra will share with other students," followed by other information.

In sum, HCSBS scores can play an important role in the design, implementation, monitoring, and evaluation of social-behavioral interventions. For more specific details on the use of the HCSBS and other behavior assessment tools in the intervention process, test users are referred to three additional works by the senior author of the HCSBS (Merrell, 2000a, 2008; Merrell &

Gimpel, 1998). Numerous other works are also available to provide information on the process of developing appropriate behavior intervention plans for children and youth that are appropriately linked to objective assessment data.

SUMMARY

A simple three-level interpretation strategy is recommended for the HCSBS. The first interpretation level involves looking at HCSBS scores in relation to their specific place or position in the norming sample, using T-scores and percentile ranks, and making some generalizations about a child or youth's scores based on their normative placement. The second interpretation level involves identifying the SFLs that correspond to HCSBS subscale and total scores and considering the possible meaning of scores at these general functional levels. The third interpretation level involves follow-up of individual HCSBS items in cases where At-Risk or High Risk levels are indicated and qualitatively inspecting these items to determine which Social Competence items are rated as never or almost never occurring and which Antisocial Behavior items are rated as occurring frequently. The two case studies presented in this chapter help illustrate the process of this tri-level interpretation strategy. Whenever possible, it is recommended that HCSBS ratings be used in a cross-informant manner so that an aggregated picture of a child or adolescent's social-behavioral functioning will be obtained. The HCSBS may be a useful tool in the initial stages of FBA, especially when it is used for generating initial hypotheses about social-behavioral functioning and followed with direct behavioral observation. Behavior rating scales such as the HCSBS and SSBS-2 may be useful in determining which children or youth may benefit from specially designed interventions, what the specific focus of these interventions should be, and how to evaluate change during and following intervention.

DEVELOPMENT, STANDARDIZATION, AND NORMATIVE INFORMATION 4

Development of the HCSBS, how the norming sample data were collected and standardized, and the general characteristics of the norming sample are detailed in this chapter. The information presented in this chapter includes instrument development procedures, data collection procedures, and descriptive information regarding the characteristics of the norming sample, including geographical representation, race and ethnicity, socioeconomic status, special education classification, age, and gender. The procedures for developing score conversion tables are also discussed. This descriptive information is supplemented in some instances with data from statistical analyses to provide additional details. These analyses were conducted to ensure that the norming procedures resulted in a final sample that is broadly similar to the population that it is intended to represent, to increase confidence in the generalization of inferences drawn from the norming sample data.

HCSBS DEVELOPMENT PROCEDURES

The HCSBS was developed to provide a cross-informant companion instrument to the original SSBS. The SSBS was designed specifically for screening and assessing the social and antisocial behavior of students in K–12 educational settings and was designed to be completed by teachers and other education professionals. Soon after the SSBS was published, the need for a cross-informant version of the instrument that could be used by parent raters and other home- and community-based informants became apparent due to numerous requests for such a tool.

The first research version of the HCSBS rating form was developed by evaluating each item of the original SSBS and modifying these items as appropriate to reflect home and community, rather than school, contexts for social and antisocial behavior. In developing the HCSBS, the authors intended to retain the same general contents and structure and to tap the same underlying theoretical constructs as the SSBS so that the two measures would be considered companion measurement tools within the same social behavior rating system. The general rule followed in developing HCSBS items was to make modifications in wording only when they were necessary to reflect differences between home/community and school contexts for social and antisocial behavior. The original research version of the HCSBS was developed by modifying 11 and retaining 21 of the 32 Social Competence items of the SSBS and modifying 12 and retaining 21 of the 33 Antisocial Behavior items. Thus, about two out of three items from the original SSBS were generic enough with regard to the context or setting indicated that they did not require modification. During the processes of norming, standardization, and final production of the HCSBS, the wording of a few of the items that had previously been modified from the SSBS underwent very slight additional changes based on feedback from raters and from the authors' colleagues.

ORIGINAL DEVELOPMENT PROCEDURES FOR THE SSBS

Because the HCSBS items were derived from the original SSBS, it is useful to review the steps that were taken to develop the SSBS, to better understand the lineage and focus of the HCSBS. This information is available in more detail in the SSBS-2 user's guide (Merrell, 2002). The development of the SSBS was theory driven, based on the notion that students in educational settings must make two forms of social adjustment (teacher-related social adjustment and peer-related social adjustment) and that consequent social behaviors tend to be either positive (social competence) or negative (antisocial problem behavior) and produce differing outcomes for students. With respect to antisocial behavior, it was also posited that a valid rating scale would need to reflect both overt and covert forms of antisocial behavior. Therefore, the SSBS, and subsequently the HCSBS, were aimed squarely at these constructs. For the HCSBS, it is appropriate to substitute the term *adult-related social adjustment* for *teacher-related social adjustment* because of the difference between home/community and school contexts.

The theoretical underpinnings of the SSBS were based on evidence from the literature on social and antisocial behavior. It was theorized that the most effective way to develop a social behavior rating scale along these lines was to include separate scales for social competence and antisocial behavior domains and to include behaviors that tap teacher-related and peer-related social adjustment within each domain. The development of SSBS items reflecting teacher-related and peer-related forms of social adjustment was not intended to be a template for SSBS subscale development. These two forms of social adjustment were reflected in the SSBS item development so that the resulting instrument would sample a broad range of child and adolescent social behaviors that were relevant to the actual types of social demands faced by children and youth in school settings.

Four steps were followed during the development of SSBS items and the SSBS rating form. These four steps are detailed as follows.

Step 1: Item Development

Because it was intended that the scale would measure social competence and antisocial problem behavior, behavioral descriptors relevant to each area were compiled through the following three primary methods: 1) through examination of the literature on social competence and antisocial behavior of children and youth, particularly as related to school settings; 2) by examining the contents of social skills training curricula and problem behavior intervention programs; and 3) through examination of existing social skills and behavior rating scales. This initial process led to the development of approximately 60 behavioral descriptors in the social competence domain and approximately 50 behavioral descriptors in the antisocial behavior domain.

Step 2: Item Refinement and Reduction

After the initial lists of social and antisocial behavioral descriptors were compiled, these lists were examined carefully by the authors and colleagues for the purpose of eliminating item duplication and to ensure that items were not identical replications of existing test items. Following these reduction procedures, approximately 50 behavioral descriptors remained in the social competence domain, and approximately 40 behavioral descriptors remained in the antisocial behavior domain.

Step 3: Content Validation

Following the process of item refinement and reduction, the remaining list of behavioral descriptors was viewed by several teachers, graduate students in psychology and education, and parents with children in the K–12 grade range. After the authors received feedback from these individuals regarding item content and wording, several items were rewritten, several items were eliminated, and additional items were added. The final revision included a total of 65 items: 32 items used in the Social Competence scale and 33 items used in the Antisocial Behavior scale. These are the items that appeared on the original SSBS rating form, although one of the Antisocial Behavior items was dropped for the SSBS-2. Both the HCSBS and the SSBS-2 do not include the item *Unproductive; achieves very little* because it was not considered to be theoretically consistent enough with the construct of antisocial behavior, even though this item held up well in psychometric analyses.

Step 4: Item Rating Format

Following extensive analyses of existing behavior rating scales and the literature on scale development and measurement issues, the rating format for the SSBS items was developed. A five-point rating format (ranging from 1 = Never to 5 = Frequently, with the descriptor Sometimes added at the mid-point of 3) was selected for the SSBS rather than a three-point rating format, which is often used by developers of behavior rating scales. The primary advantage considered in selecting the five-point rating format over a three-point format was that the five-point format allows for finer or more sensitive differentiation of how often various behaviors occur. The five-point scale, however, is still short enough that it can be completed quickly and reliably by raters. This rating scale development process is consistent with the recommendation of experts in educational and psychological measurement, who contend that the best rating formats are those that allow for a sensitive differentiation of the item response but are not so complicated that they are difficult to complete (Worthen, Borg, & White, 1993). The HCSBS and SSBS-2 also use this five-point rating scale.

In sum, the steps taken to develop the contents and rating format for the SSBS, and subsequently the HCSBS, were carefully conducted, theory driven, and based on a solid foundation of scientific evidence. Great care was also taken to ensure that the resulting items and rating format would be easy to use and intuitive. The result of this careful work over several years was a unique and innovative set of behavior rating scales.

DATA COLLECTION PROCEDURES

Data collection for the HCSBS norming and standardization sample began with a small item tryout and psychometric study in 1995 and 1996. The majority of the data collection was conducted between 1998 and 2001. The authors of the HCSBS and colleagues relied on several methods to recruit data collection sites, including direct mail recruitment flyers to individuals randomly selected from the directory of Nationally Certified School Psychologists, personal contacts, and recruitment of public school districts where there were institutional contacts in place. For the most part, the authors relied on public school personnel to coordinate data collection efforts from parents and guardians of their students. Individuals who expressed interest in coordinating data collection efforts through their school systems were provided with data collection packets, which included rating scales, sample instructions to be given to teachers, and detailed instructions for the individuals who were coordinating data collection at each site.

Data collection was conducted with the approval of human subjects institutional review boards at Utah State University (from 1995 to 1996) and the University of Iowa (from 1998 through 2001), where the senior author was professionally affiliated during the norm-gathering time period. In cases where recruitment of parent raters was conducted through public school districts, administrative approval from the sponsoring district was also obtained. Potential parent or guardian raters for the norming sample were presented with research packets, requests to participate, and consent forms. The research packets included directions, space to enter demographic information on children and adolescents who were being rated, the HCSBS rating forms, and in some cases, comparison measures for the validity studies. The method of data collection did not personally identify raters or the children and youth who were rated. Completed research packets were returned to the research site coordinators or mailed directly to the authors of the HCSBS.

DEVELOPMENT, STANDARDIZATION, AND NORMATIVE INFORMATION 41

Data collection for the norming and standardization research resulted in a return of more than 2,000 useable HCSBS research forms from 13 communities in 9 U.S. states. The final norming sample of 1,562 cases was selected from this larger pool using randomized block procedures to ensure a sample that was generally representative of the U.S. population in terms of race/ethnicity, socioeconomic status, gender, and general/special education classification status.

CHARACTERISTICS OF THE NORMING SAMPLE

This section provides an overview of the general characteristics of the HCSBS norming sample, including raters, community and geographic region, race and ethnicity, socioeconomic status, special education status, age, and gender.

Raters

Raters were asked on the data collection forms to describe their relationship to the child or adolescent whom they were rating. Of the 1,562 cases in the final norming sample, mothers comprised the largest group of raters (70.1%), followed by individuals who identified themselves as "other" on the data collection forms (10.6%), fathers (9.9%), stepmothers (1.2%), grandmothers (1.1%), stepfathers (.4%), and grandfathers (.2%). In 6.5% of the cases, the rater did not identify his or her relationship to the child or adolescent. The 10.6% of raters who identified themselves as "other" were presumably foster parents, legal guardians, group home supervisors, and older siblings or other family members in a quasicustodial role.

Communities, States, and Geographic Regions

As indicated in Table 4.1, the HCSBS norming sample includes ratings of 1,562 children and youth representing 12 communities, 10 states, and each of the 4 major U.S. geographic regions (West, North Central, Northeast, and South). The communities represented in the norming sample represent a mix of urban, suburban, and rural areas.

As these data indicate, the sample is weighted toward the West and North Central regions and, to a lesser extent, the South region. Only a small percentage of cases (5%) are from the Northeast region. Although the norm sample is not perfectly balanced with respect to geographical region, it is important to recognize that unlike cognitive tests (i.e., intelligence tests and academic achievement tests), which are known to produce scores that tend to differ systematically across regions of the United States, no systematic regional effect has been found for behavior rating scale scores (Merrell, 2000b). Therefore, there is no theoretical or empirical reason to believe that the modest geographical imbalance in the HCSBS norming sample should pose a threat to the

Table 4.1. Communities represented by the 1,562 cases in the final norming sample, listed by community type and divided by the four primary U.S. geographic regions

West (n = 719; 46%)	North Central (n = 446; 29%)	Northeast (n = 78; 5%)	South (n = 319; 20%)
Cedar City, UT	Cedar Rapids, IA	Grantsville, WV	Hobe Sound, FL
Roslyn/Cle Elum, WA	Fox Lake, IL	Providence, RI	Little Rock, AR
Ogden, UT			Richmond, VA
Safford, AZ			
Tacoma, WA			

validity or generalizability of scores. In fact, randomly selected cases from each region (matched by gender, age, and special education status) were analyzed to investigate any possible regional effects, and the differences in mean scores were all within the standard error of measurement (SEM) of the test.

Race and Ethnicity

During the norming and standardization process for the HCSBS, raters were asked to provide basic demographic information on the students they rated, including identification of the racial or ethnic group with which they presumed the student was identified. Based on this information, the norming sample reflects a highly diverse group of children and youth in terms of race and ethnicity. Table 4.2 presents the percentages of cases in the norming sample in each of the major racial or ethnic groups in the United States (listed by U.S. Census Bureau categories). In addition, information on the percentage of cases in each of these groups from the 2000 U.S. Census is provided for comparison purposes. Children and youth in the final norming sample of 1,562 cases were identified as 71.3% White/Caucasian, 13.5% Black/African American, 10.8% Hispanic, 1.7% Asian or Pacific Islander, 0.4% American Indian, Eskimo, or Aleut (Native American), and 2% described as multiracial or other on the research forms.

These data indicate that the racial/ethnic makeup of the final norming sample is diverse and that most of the major racial/ethnic groups are represented in the norming sample at a rate similar to their proportional representation in the general U.S. population. The three largest groups, White/Caucasian, African American, and Hispanic, are all represented in the norming sample within no more than 1.3% difference from their proportionality in the general U.S. population. The Asian American (Asian or Pacific Islander) and Native American (American Indian, Eskimo, or Aleut) are both somewhat underrepresented in the norming sample, which is an artifact of the population base in the communities from where the norming sample was drawn. Significant efforts were undertaken during the development of the HCSBS to make the sample as representative of the 2000 U.S. Census as possible.

With respect to child behavior rating scale norming samples in general, there is some evidence indicating that ethnicity is not a critical factor in influ-

Table 4.2. Racial/ethnic composition of HCSBS standardization sample, listed by percentages, in comparison to general U.S. population

Racial/ethnic group	Percentage in HCSBS standardization sample	Percentage in general U.S. population*
White/Caucasian	71.30%	71.50%
Black/African American	13.50%	12.20%
Hispanic	10.80%	11.80%
Asian and Pacific Islander	1.70%	3.80%
American Indian, Eskimo, and Aleut	0.40%	0.70%
Multiracial/Other	2.00%	NA

Source: U.S. Census Bureau, Population Estimates Program, Population Division. (2001, July 2). *Resident population estimates of the United States by sex, race, and Hispanic origin: Short-term projection to July 1, 2000.* Washington, DC: Author. Available online at http://www.census.gov/population/estimates/nation/intfile3-1.txt

encing scores, especially if the effects of social class or socioeconomic status are controlled (Achenbach & Edelbrock, 1981; Merrell, 2000b). In fact, although there is a paucity of research in this area, the current best empirical evidence indicates that over- or underrepresentation of specific ethnic groups of participants in educational and psychological test norm samples is not a critical factor in influencing group differences in scores (Fan, Wilson, & Kapes, 1996). Rather, the reliability and validity of the assessment instrument for use with particular groups appears to be the critical issue in this regard. If an assessment instrument is equally valid and reliable for members of various ethnic groups, then minor over- or underrepresentation of these groups in the norm sample should not influence the stability or usefulness of scores.

Because the item development procedures for the HCSBS and SSBS were based on the existing literature and empirical evidence regarding presentation of social competence and antisocial behavior in children and adolescents, these instruments should be useful across varying ethnic groups within the United States and potentially in other nations in which English is the most common language. There is, however, always the possibility that cultural and linguistic factors may influence assessment results in ways that may adversely affect the individual who is being assessed, particularly if an individual who is being rated is not well integrated into the mainstream culture. If potential test users suspect that the HCSBS items or norms may not be appropriate for a student from a specific racial, ethnic, or cultural group (e.g., a recent immigrant to the United States from a nation with widely differing social-behavioral norms), then this instrument should be used with great caution.

Socioeconomic Status

Socioeconomic status is a complex construct that is generally considered to be reflected by a variety of indicators, including family income, education level, social class, occupation, and social and political views (Appelbaum & Chambliss, 1997). Socioeconomic status of the norming sample was estimated through determining parent occupational categories. As they completed the research packets, parent raters were asked to list their occupations. In cases where the rater was someone other than a parent of the target child, the rater was asked to list the occupation of the child's parents. Parental occupation was selected as the target socioeconomic indicator for two reasons. First, it would be more readily known and potentially less invasive to raters than other measures of socioeconomic status such as annual family income, parents' educational level, or eligibility for free or reduced-price school lunch programs. Second, there is a considerable body of evidence from the field of sociology that occupational category is linked strongly to social class and socialization (Appelbaum & Chambliss, 1997; Kohn & Schooler, 1983; Stanley & Baca-Zinn, 1997).

Parent occupational data were coded and collapsed into eight general occupational categories, based on categorical breakdowns that have been used previously by the U.S. Department of Labor and which have been used for previous social science research on occupation and social class. In cases where occupations were listed for two parents and their occupations fell into more than one coding category, the occupational category that was considered to be linked to higher socioeconomic status was coded.

Based on these general categorical divisions, the estimated percentages of occupational categories for parents of children and youth in the norming sample are provided in Table 4.3. As these data indicate, the parents of children and youth who were rated for the norming sample were from varied occupational and socioeconomic backgrounds. It is difficult to compare these percentages to the occupational categories of the general U.S. population for various reasons, including the lack of a specific and standard occupational metric by which occupational data are compiled by governmental agencies and the

Table 4.3. Occupational status of parents of children and youth in HCSBS norming sample, listed by general categories and percentages

Occupational category	Percent
Agriculture, forestry, fishing, and related occupations	1.4%
Unemployed	3.7%
Unknown or not listed	4.5%
Sales and related occupations	7.3%
Clerical and administrative support positions	7.3%
Production, construction, operating, maintenance, and material handling occupations	12.4%
Service occupations	12.9%
Managerial and administrative occupations	18.1%
Professional, paraprofessional, and technical occupations	32.6%

constantly changing nature of the American economy and work force; however, some general inferences about the sample can be made based on data that is available from the Bureau of Labor Statistics web site (located at http://www.bls.gov/) and other information from the U.S. Department of Labor (including the *Occupational Outlook Handbook*). It appears that the parents of children and youth whose behavior ratings comprise the HCSBS norming sample differed slightly from the general U.S. population in three ways: They were slightly less likely to be employed in jobs that fall into the *Agriculture, forestry, fishing, and related occupations* category; they were slightly less likely to be unemployed; and they were moderately more likely to work in jobs that fell into the *Professional, paraprofessional, and technical occupations* category. Aside from these three areas, occupational differences between the HCSBS norming sample and the general U.S. population are not remarkable.

In sum, it can be inferred that the children and youth who comprised the HCSBS norming sample are from a diversity of socioeconomic backgrounds. Based on occupational category, parents of these children and youth were found to be reasonably comparable to the general U.S. population. This socioeconomic status estimate provides further support for the comparability of the sample to the general U.S. population.

Special Education Participation

One of the goals for development of the HCSBS was for the final norming sample to include a similar range of students with disabilities and students who receive special education as found in the general population of the United States. During the data collection and norm-gathering research, raters were asked to provide information on any known disabilities of the target child or youth, as well as the child or youth's participation in special education programs at school. These data were coded according to the standard disability and service classification categories used in American schools based on the criteria from the Individuals with Disabilities Education Act of 1990 (PL 101-476). Disability and special education classification status were both used as target matching and blocking variables during the process of narrowing the initial norming sample of more than 2,000 to the final norming sample of 1,562.

The special education participation rates and disability classification categories of the final HCSBS norming sample are presented in Table 4.4. As these data indicate, the norming sample is virtually identical to the general U.S. population of children and youth with respect to these characteristics, based on comparison information from the U.S. Department of Education (2000). The total disability or special education participation rate of 11.70% for the norming sample is very close to the 12.80% comparison figure from the general U.S. student population, and the differences between the norming sample and the general population estimates are less than 1%.

Table 4.4. Special education participation percentages by disability classification categories of the norming sample, with comparison percentages from general U.S. student population

Special education category	Percent in norm sample	Percent in U.S. population*
Learning disability	5.90%	5.91%
Speech or language impairments	2.10%	2.30%
Mental retardation	1.20%	1.28%
Emotional disturbance	1.10%	0.98%
Other disabilities	1.40%	2.33%
All disabilities	11.70%	12.80%

Source: U.S. Department of Education, National Center for Education Statistics. (2000). Children 0-21 years old served in federally supported programs for the disabled, by type of disability: 1976-77 to 1997-98. *Digest of Education Statistics.* Available at http://nces.ed.gov/pubs2000/Digest99/d99t053.html

Age

Age breakdowns for the norming sample, as well as means and standard deviations by age for the Social Competence Total and Antisocial Behavior Total scores, are presented in Tables 4.5 and 4.6, respectively. These data are presented along with gender data. There are comparable numbers of boys and girls at each age level, but the total number of cases at each age level does vary somewhat, with fewer cases for ages 5 and 18. The lower number of cases at these age levels is a logical reflection of how age is distributed at K–12 school grade levels.

To evaluate the relationship of age to HCSBS scores, the subscale and total scores of the entire standardization sample were correlated with age, using the bivariate Pearson product-moment correlation procedure. The resulting coefficients from this analysis are presented in Table 4.7. In general, the HCSBS score correlations with age are quite weak, ranging from –.11 to .10 and often approach the zero level. All coefficients, however, were statistically significant at the $p < .01$ level, a finding that is mostly attributable to the large sample size. The general direction and strength of these coefficients indicate that as age increases, Social Competence scores increase slightly and Antisocial Behavior scores decrease slightly.

To evaluate age effects in more detail, means and standard deviations for the total scale scores were computed, and these values were compared and contrasted according to the intended age breakdown for the HCSBS norming samples: ages 5–11 and 12–18. The resulting descriptive statistics were as follows: For the Social Competence Total score, the 5–11 age group had a mean score of 120.77 with a standard deviation of 23.32, whereas the 12–18 age group had a mean score of 125.04 with a standard deviation of 22.78. For the Antisocial Behavior Total score, the 5–11 age group had a mean score of 58.92 with a standard deviation of 21.07, whereas the 12–18 age group had a mean score of 55.77 with a standard deviation of 21.80. Contrasts of these scores were made using the standard effect size (ES) estimation method recom-

Table 4.5. Raw score means and standard deviations for Social Competence Total score, by age and gender, for entire HCSBS norming sample

	Boys			Girls			All*		
Age	N	M	SD	N	M	SD	N	M	SD
5	21	113.10	20.40	23	128.40	13.28	45	121.30	18.39
6	59	115.53	25.00	22	126.20	16.99	82	118.70	23.44
7	45	117.27	20.60	31	130.20	24.59	80	123.11	23.23
8	45	113.67	24.07	53	124.90	21.84	99	119.84	23.34
9	51	117.41	27.98	54	122.40	27.11	108	120.10	27.35
10	48	114.35	24.06	35	127.50	16.46	83	119.90	20.06
11	48	117.52	22.36	68	126.00	21.61	119	122.51	22.10
12	60	123.65	20.75	91	127.30	20.98	154	125.04	22.17
13	112	119.31	23.74	97	131.40	16.64	210	124.79	21.60
14	88	118.38	25.67	76	128.10	23.80	165	122.90	25.15
15	73	120.68	26.55	84	127.90	19.48	160	124.82	23.13
16	65	125.22	21.30	38	132.60	20.81	105	127.56	21.25
17	52	125.83	25.44	52	128.00	24.30	105	126.10	25.12
18	21	124.24	18.18	25	128.90	18.37	47	126.31	17.99

Note: The sum of Boys and Girls cases does not equal All due to cases for which gender was not indicated on the HCSBS research form.

Key: N, total number in sample; M, mean; SD, standard deviation.

Table 4.6. Raw score means and standard deviations for Antisocial Behavior Total Score, by age and gender, for entire HCSBS norming sample

	Boys			Girls			All		
Age	N	M	SD	N	M	SD	N	M	SD
5	21	57.11	20.10	23	55.70	13.78	45	56.10	16.81
6	59	62.34	24.92	22	57.32	13.01	82	60.80	22.32
7	45	60.10	20.22	31	56.60	21.20	80	58.10	20.31
8	45	70.11	28.69	53	53.80	15.90	99	61.30	23.92
9	51	55.91	19.10	54	59.11	21.93	108	58.10	21.11
10	48	59.10	19.72	35	56.00	20.34	83	57.80	19.94
11	48	63.40	22.01	68	55.89	19.67	119	58.82	20.73
12	60	53.01	19.10	91	54.20	19.10	154	54.94	21.65
13	112	63.91	27.75	97	52.01	15.74	210	58.43	23.64
14	88	60.59	24.72	76	53.09	20.61	165	56.93	23.10
15	73	59.91	25.20	84	52.20	19.64	160	55.62	22.60
16	65	54.50	17.43	38	49.53	21.17	105	52.80	18.82
17	52	55.53	17.29	52	52.91	22.51	105	54.50	20.23
18	21	54.61	14.48	25	50.83	15.49	47	53.01	15.10

Note: The sum of Boys and Girls cases does not equal All due to cases for which gender was not indicated on the HCSBS research form.

Key: N, total number in sample; M, mean; SD, standard deviation.

mended by Cohen (1988), which is also referred to as *Cohen's D*. For the Social Competence Total score, the resulting ES was .18, which is lower than the minimum .20 recommended by Cohen as indicating any practical meaning and demonstrating less than one fifth of a standard deviation difference between the groups. For the Antisocial Behavior Total score, the resulting ES was .14, even lower than that of the Social Competence score.

Table 4.7. Correlations between HCSBS scores and age, grade level, and gender for the HCSBS national norming sample

HCSBS scales	Age	Grade	Gender
Peer Relations	.07	.08	.17
Self-Management/Compliance	.10	.11	.17
Social Competence Total	.09	.10	.18
Defiant/Disruptive	−.11	−.12	−.09
Antisocial/Aggressive	−.04	−.05	−.15
Antisocial Behavior Total	−.08	−.09	−.12

Note: All correlations are significant at $p < .01$.

Although there are some minor trends of increasing Social Competence scores and decreasing Antisocial Behavior scores with increased age, the effects of age in relation to the HCSBS appear to be weak, and there is not a meaningful pattern of age groupings in terms of statistical power. Based on these findings, a case could be made that it was not necessary to divide the HCSBS norm sample into norming subsamples. Most parents, teachers, and clinicians, however, are accustomed to making comparisons of a given child's test scores with those of their general age group, and such grouping divisions are quite common on behavior rating scales. Therefore, a decision was made to divide the norming sample into 5–11 and 12–18 age subsamples for purposes of raw score conversions and normative comparisons. This division was made for the ease and comfort level of test users, as well as for similarity to other measures that may be used with the HCSBS.

Gender

Gender breakdowns for the norming sample, as well as means and standard deviations by gender and age level for the Social Competence Total and Antisocial Behavior Total scores, are presented in Tables 4.5 and 4.6. These data are presented along with age range data. There are comparable numbers of boys and girls at each age level and overall. Note that the sum of the number of boys and girls does not equal "All" cases for each row. This discrepancy can be explained by the fact that a small number of research cases that were used in the norming sample did not provide gender identification information for the child or adolescent who was rated.

To explore the effect of gender on HCSBS scores, Spearman's rho correlations were computed between the categorical variable of gender (1 = male, 2 = female) and the HCSBS scale and subscale scores. The Spearman's rho correlation method was used because it is more appropriate in situations where one of the variables in the correlation matrix is categorical rather than continuous. The correlation coefficients from this analysis are presented in Table 4.7, along with the correlations between age and HCSBS scores. The obtained correlations range from −.15 to .18, and although slightly stronger than the correlations between scores and age, are still quite weak. Because of the way that gender was coded in the data files, the general direction of these findings indicate that Social Competence scores tended to increase slightly for girls and decrease slightly for boys, whereas Antisocial Behavior scores showed the reverse pattern. Although statistically significant, these correlations are still quite weak, and the statistical significance can be explained in part as a result of the large sample size. Cohen (1988), in his classic text on the practical meaning of statistical power, argued that correlations of less than .20 should be generally considered as having no practical meaning or significance, even if they are statistically significant, because they reflect 4% or less in terms of shared variance among the two scores in the correlation.

To examine the relationship between gender and HCSBS scores in more detail, the mean scores of boys and girls for the entire norming sample were contrasted using a T-test for independent means (with unequal variances assumed). For the Social Competence Total score, the average score of girls (M = 127.76, SD = 21.05) was significantly higher than that of boys (M = 119.29, SD = 24.03): t (1524.95) = -7.36, $p < .001$, indicating that girls were rated as having an overall significantly better level of social competence than boys. A follow-up ES calculation using Cohen's D method produced an ES of .37, which indicates slightly more than one third of a standard deviation difference between the average score of girls and boys and is considered to be meaningful but small. For the Antisocial Behavior Total score, the average score of girls (M = 53.93, SD = 19.08) was significantly lower than that of boys (M = 59.74, SD = 23.01): t (1505.43) = 5.40, $p < .001$, indicating that girls were rated overall as having significantly fewer antisocial behaviors than boys. An ES of .28 was obtained between these scores, indicating a difference of slightly more than one fourth of a standard deviation between the average score of boys and girls. Like the ES estimates for the Social Competence Total score, this ES is considered to be meaningful but small.

Although these findings of significant (albeit modest) gender differences in HCSBS scores might seem to argue in favor of developing separate norming samples based on gender, this approach was rejected for both practical and theoretical reasons. It is no surprise that girls in the norming sample were found to have an overall better level of social-behavioral adjustment than boys. This finding replicates a general trend in the literature over many years (see Merrell & Gimpel, 1998, for a thorough review of gender differences in social behavior). In fact, these gender differences present evidence supporting the construct validity of the HCSBS and are thus addressed in more detail in Chapter 6. There is, however, no compelling reason to use separate score norms for girls and boys because these gender differences are expected and do not disadvantage or bias either group when it comes to their test results. In fact, the use of same-gender norms in this situation could very likely result in overidentification of some girls as having social competence deficits and antisocial behavior deficits when they in fact do not exhibit these deficits (a false-positive error) and underidentification of some boys who actually do have significant social-behavioral deficits (a false-negative error). Given this line of reasoning, the norming subsamples are not divided by gender.

In school settings, student behavior (and subsequent screening for intervention or special placement) is typically based on how compatible that behavior is with overall school rules and expectations, rather than how compatible it is with what is typical for boys or girls; however, clinicians who may be interested in making detailed comparisons of the HCSBS scores of specific individuals based on gender may consult the descriptive statistics in Tables 4.5 and 4.6. Caution is advised in making comparisons between scores of individual children or youth and their gender or grade average scores because in some cases the number of norm sample cases in particular cells are relatively small when broken down in this manner. Such small numbers may not adequately represent the gender and grade-level characteristics desired and may be "sample-dependent." It is recommended that the score conversion tables in Appendix A and Appendix B generally be used for normative comparison purposes.

DEVELOPMENT OF SCORE CONVERSION TABLES

After the decision was made to divide the final norming samples into two subsamples based on age groupings (5–11 and 12–18), raw score frequencies and percentile ranks for the subscale and total scores were computed for each age group. The raw scores for each of the 12 resulting score distributions (6 distributions for each of the 2 age groups, based on 2 subscale scores and 1 total score for each of the two scales) were then converted to T-scores, using the following formula:

$$T = \frac{X - M}{SD} \times 10 + 50$$

In this example, X is the specific raw score being converted to a T-score, M is the mean raw score from the raw score distribution, and SD is the standard deviation for the raw score distribution.

T-scores are standard scores based on a normative mean of 50 and standard deviation of 10. As is discussed in Chapter 3, the HCSBS T-scores are based on linear transformations of raw scores. They are not normalized or "smoothed" to approximate a perfectly "bell-shaped" distribution of scores but reflect the actual and slightly skewed score distributions that were found with the norming samples.

Development of the Spanish-Language HCSBS Rating Form

Translation of the HCSBS rating form into Spanish was accomplished through the efforts of four translators, all of whom were bilingual in both Spanish and English. Two of the translators were native English speakers and two were native Spanish speakers. After the development of what the authors considered to be a near-final translation process, the Spanish-language form was reviewed by two additional bilingual experts (one professor of Spanish and one professor of psychology, who were both native Spanish speakers) and some minor final corrections were made. The Spanish-language HCSBS rating form is intended for use by native Spanish speakers within the United States. Because of dialectal differences in use of Spanish across various regions of the world, some of the items may use phrasing that may not be typical in all Spanish dialects, but it was designed for utility across the major dialects of Spanish used in the United States. The same scoring procedures and norm sample are used for both versions of the HCSBS.

SUMMARY

The HCSBS was developed using a theory-driven construction of relevant behavioral descriptors into two separate general scales. The HCSBS items reflect the most critical forms of social adjustment that are required of children and youth in home, school, and community settings, as well as covert and overt antisocial behaviors. Great care was undertaken during the development of the instrument to ensure strong content validity and technical properties. The HCSBS norming sample is similar to the racial or ethnic characteristics of the general U.S. population, based on the 2000 U.S. Census data. The norming group represents a geographically diverse population whose socioeconomic and educational classification makeup is very similar to that of the general U.S. population. The HCSBS should be considered to be generally applicable and useful for children and adolescents from across the United States, and it may have applications in other nations as well. The recommended normative breakdown by 5–11 and 12–18 age levels, representing both boys and girls, provides a practical and psychometrically sound base for making normative comparisons of HCSBS scores. The score conversion tables found in Appendix A and Appendix B were developed using these carefully considered norming group breakdowns and are based on linear transformations of HCSBS raw scores to *T*-scores.

RELIABILITY OF THE HCSBS   5

Reliability of an assessment tool is defined as the *consistency or stability* of its scores when it is administered to a population of individuals or groups (AERA, APA, & NCME, 1999). *Test reliability* has been defined more specifically as how well the scores generalize across three major domains: differing item samples, differing times of administration, and differing scorers (Gregory, 2000; Salvia & Ysseldyke, 2000). Reliability is a cornerstone aspect of measurement. In the absence of adequate reliability, there can be no validity. In practice, the most common types of reliability are referred to as *internal consistency*, *test–retest*, and *interrater*, reliability. In addition, the SEM of a test is directly related to the consistency or stability of measurement because it provides information regarding how much error is likely to be present in test scores. Each of these reliability indicators has been investigated for the HCSBS. This chapter provides the details and results of the analyses that have been conducted to investigate the reliability of the scales and presents these reliability data for evaluation and future reference.

INTERNAL CONSISTENCY RELIABILITY

Internal consistency reliability is a term that refers to how stable or consistent the scores of a measure are within that measure. The two most common methods of determining internal consistency reliability, namely Cronbach's (1951) coefficient alpha and the Spearman-Brown split-half reliability procedure, were computed using data from the entire HCSBS standardization sample, as well as for the samples used to develop the norming samples for ages 5–11 and 12–18. These two procedures both provide measures of internal stability but differ because the alpha procedure is based on intercorrelations of all comparable parts of the same test, whereas the split-half procedure divides the test into two equivalent halves and estimates the consistency between "forms."

As the data in Table 5.1 indicate, both of these reliability estimation methods produced high coefficients of internal consistency across samples. These data all indicate that the HCSBS has very strong internal stability. For the total scores of the two major scales, the alpha and split-half coefficients range from .94 to .97 across the three samples. The alpha and split-half coefficients for the four subscales range from .91 to .95 and are all well above the minimum levels of acceptability recommended by Salvia and Ysseldyke

54 HCSBS USER'S GUIDE

Table 5.1. Internal consistency of HCSBS scores: alpha and split-half reliability coefficients

HCSBS Scales	Ages 5–11 (N = 616)		Ages 12–18 (N = 946)		Total sample (N = 1,562)	
	Alpha	Split-Half	Alpha	Split-Half	Alpha	Split-Half
Peer Relations	.95	.93	.95	.93	.94	.93
Self-Management/Compliance	.94	.91	.94	.92	.94	.92
Social Competence Total	.97	.95	.97	.95	.97	.95
Defiant/Disruptive	.93	.91	.94	.94	.94	.93
Antisocial/Aggressive	.93	.92	.94	.92	.94	.92
Antisocial Behavior Total	.96	.94	.97	.95	.96	.94

Key: N, total number in sample.

(2000) for measures that are to be used to make important decisions such as placement and program eligibility. The slightly lower coefficients of internal consistency for the subscale scores, as opposed to the total scores, reflects the fact that internal consistency reliability is positively related to the number of items in a test (Gregory, 2000; Salvia & Ysseldyke, 2000).

These data indicate that the internal reliability of all scales of the HCSBS across each of the norming samples and the total sample is uniformly and exceptionally strong. The internal consistency of the HCSBS exceeds the minimum recommended levels by a substantial margin.

STANDARD ERROR OF MEASUREMENT

The SEM of an assessment tool is closely related to its internal stability. The internal consistency coefficient is used in calculating the SEM (by multiplying the standard deviation by the square root of 1 minus the internal consistency coefficient), and as the coefficient of internal consistency decreases, the SEM increases. Unlike the coefficient of internal consistency, which is not helpful in directly interpreting individual scores, the SEM is useful in determining the limits of a *true score.*

SEMs are often used in constructing *confidence intervals* around which test scores may be interpreted. The SEM is based on the assumption that any *obtained score* consists of both a *true score* and an *error score* (the amount of error or unreliability that is present in the test) (Gregory, 2000; Salvia & Ysseldyke, 2000). The SEM provides a band of error that can be placed around a test score to provide a range within which the true score is likely to fall. In other words, it tells us how close a person's obtained score is to his or her true score, or the score that he or she would have obtained if a test could be completely error free.

Using the alpha coefficients presented in Table 5.1, SEMs were calculated for the subscale and total scores of the entire standardization sample, as well as the two norming subsamples. The resulting SEMs are presented in Table 5.2. The SEMs for HCSBS scores are small and indicate that the range of error surrounding obtained scores is minimal. For example, for the Social Competence Total score of the 5–11 norming sample, the SEM of 4.04 is

Table 5.2. Standard error of measurement of HCSBS scores

HCSBS Scales	SEM		
	Ages 5-11 (N = 616)	Ages 12-18 (N = 946)	Total Sample (N = 1,562)
Peer Relations	2.91	2.79	3.11
Self-Management/Compliance	2.82	2.83	2.84
Social Competence Total	4.04	3.95	4.01
Defiant/Disruptive	3.03	2.88	2.86
Antisocial/Aggressive	2.75	2.64	2.61
Antisocial Behavior Total	4.21	3.78	4.31

Key: N, total number in sample; *SEM*, standard error of measurement.

equivalent to only 17% of the raw score standard deviation, and for the Antisocial Behavior Total score, the SEM of 4.21 was equivalent to approximately 19% of the raw score standard deviation. Overall, these SEM calculations indicate that the band of error surrounding HCSBS scores is minimal.

TEST-RETEST RELIABILITY

Test–retest reliability indicates the stability of scores across time. Tests that purport to measure highly stable constructs such as intelligence would be expected to demonstrate very high test–retest reliability over short periods of time. Social-emotional assessment instruments are generally not expected to evidence extremely strong test–retest reliability because there is more variability across time in the construct of interest (Merrell, 2008); however, there is still significant consistency over time in the social behavior of children. It should be expected that scores from social behavior rating scales for children and youth will demonstrate a moderately high degree of stability over short periods of time and a moderate degree of stability over longer periods of time.

To evaluate the test–retest reliability of the HCSBS, a subset of raters for the national standardization sample was requested to provide an initial rating on the targeted child or adolescent, then to provide a second rating conducted 2 weeks later. A total of 137 raters participated in this retest study and provided usable matched pairs of research packets. These raters were parents or other adult family members in custodial or supervisory roles with the children and youth who were rated. The retest study was conducted entirely through the Cedar City, Utah, norming site, a rural community in Southern Utah. The children and youth who were rated ranged in age from 5 to 18 years and were nearly evenly divided between boys and girls (68 boys, 69 girls). Ethnicity of the retest sample reflected the demographic makeup of the community from which it was drawn and was 96% White. The children and youth rated were a general nonclinical sample, and only 11 out of those who were rated were identified as having a disability or a clinical disorder.

Bivariate Pearson product-moment correlations were computed between the baseline scores and the scores obtained at the 2-week retest interval. The resulting coefficients of stability, which are presented in Table 5.3, are all

Table 5.3. Test-retest reliability coefficients for HCSBS scores of 137 children and adolescents rated at 2-week intervals

HCSBS scales	Reliability coefficient
Peer Relations	.83
Self-Management/Compliance	.82
Social Competence Total	.84
Defiant/Disruptive	.91
Antisocial/Aggressive	.89
Antisocial Behavior Total	.91

Note: All coefficients are significant at $p < .001$.

quite high, ranging from .82 to .91, and are statistically significant at the $p < .001$ level. Interestingly, the test–retest coefficients for the Antisocial Behavior scale are somewhat higher than for the Social Competence scale, which may be attributable to the fact that almost all of the ratings reflected very few antisocial problem behaviors, and there was thus less potential for variability. It is an expected finding that these coefficients of stability are somewhat lower than the coefficients of internal consistency for the HCSBS; this is consistent with many other studies that have investigated the psychometric characteristics of child behavior rating scale scores. The general range of these reliability coefficients is similar to other investigations of short-term stability of child behavior rating scale scores, including studies of the original SSBS.

INTERRATER RELIABILITY

An additional type of test reliability involves consistency of measurement across differing pairs of raters or scorers. With child behavior rating scales, this type of reliability is particularly important because recommended practice in child behavior assessment dictates the development of aggregated assessment designs, including information obtained from multiple informants and based on child behavior in multiple settings. As mentioned previously, this type of aggregated and comprehensive assessment design is referred to as *multimethod, multisource, multisetting assessment design* (Merrell, 2008).

During the norming research, a study was conducted to evaluate the consistency or stability of HCSBS scores across differing raters who evaluated the same child or adolescent. This study included HCSBS scores of 83 children and youth ages 7–18 who were rated by two parents (or in a handful of cases, other custodial family members or stepparents) who were living in the same home. Some of these cases were obtained from general norming sites when both parents volunteered to complete rating packets, and other cases were recruited specifically for this reliability study. Gender breakdowns for the group of 83 children and youth were similar (43 boys, 40 girls), and this sample was 90% White. Most of the 83 youths were general education students, although a few (14) were acknowledged as having identified disabilities or disorders.

Interrater reliability coefficients for these cases were computed using bivariate Pearson product-moment correlations between ratings provided by the mother and father for each child or adolescent. These coefficients are shown in Table 5.4. The range of coefficients is .85 to .86 for the Social Competence scores, and .64 to .73 for the Antisocial Behavior scores. These correlations are in the moderate to high range and reflect slightly more stability across raters with respect to positive social behaviors. Using the data from Achenbach, McConaughy, and Howell's (1987) influential meta-analysis on cross-informant reliability, this range of coefficients is similar to or slightly higher than what might be expected based on child behavior ratings from two parents in the same setting. Overall, these data provide solid evidence of good to excellent interrater reliability.

It is interesting to note that although the correlation or association between pairs of scores is moderate to high, the variation across raters within pairs is probable in terms of individual item patterns rather than aggregated item scores (i.e., subscales and total scores). The mean Social Competence Total scores from mothers ($M = 113.34$, $SD = 29.54$) and fathers ($M = 114.112$, $SD = 30.23$) were almost identical, and the ES of .02 for the difference in these scores is virtually nil and well below the minimum .20 recommended by Cohen (1988) for an effect to be considered meaningful, even at a small level. With respect to the Antisocial Behavior Total scores, those obtained from the mothers' ratings ($M = 47.51$, $SD = 19.50$) were slightly higher than those provided by fathers ($M = 43.66$, $SD = 19.52$), but this difference is minimal, and the ES of the differences (.19) still does not reach the criterion for a meaningful difference.

In practice, interpretation of child behavior rating scales obtained from various raters is a complex process. Interrater reliability coefficients obtained with child behavior rating scales are always considerably lower than internal consistency coefficients, and they are usually lower than test–retest coefficients and alternate form coefficients (Merrell, 2000a). When two raters who observe the same child in the same setting (e.g., the child's mother and father)

Table 5.4. HCSBS interrater reliability coefficients from parent rater pairs (mothers and fathers) of 83 children and adolescents

HCSBS scales	Reliability coefficient
Peer Relations	.85
Self-Management/Compliance	.86
Social Competence Total	.86
Defiant/Disruptive	.64
Antisocial/Aggressive	.73
Antisocial Behavior Total	.71

Note: All coefficients are significant at $p < .01$.

rate the behavior of the child using a standardized behavioral rating tool, there is always some variability in the obtained ratings. One reason for this expected score variability is the fact that different raters have unique approaches to the task of providing ratings. This phenomenon has been referred to as *source bias* (Merrell, 2008); however, a more practical reason for the variability in scores among raters in the same setting is that they actually have had opportunities to observe the child's behavior in unique situations or circumstances. For example, it is widely understood that children may behave differently when they are with one parent or the other, or one teacher or another, because of the unique environmental and relationship characteristics (Kazdin, 1979; Mischel, 1968). Although some score variability is expected across child behavior raters within the same setting, interrater reliability coefficients of this type are typically moderate to moderately strong.

SUMMARY

The evidence presented in this chapter indicates that the HCSBS is a highly reliable measure. The various reliability studies presented in this chapter are consistent with or superior to the results of similar studies that have been conducted with other behavior rating scales designed for generally similar purposes. The internal consistency reliability of the HCSBS is exceptionally strong, and the SEM is quite small. The stability of HCSBS scores over short periods of time is very strong. The interrater reliability of HCSBS scores across parent raters within the same setting is strong and enhances the confidence of using this measure with multiple raters. The solid reliability evidence presented in this chapter is a necessary precursor to establishing confidence in its use for a variety of clinical, educational, and research purposes and to demonstrating various forms of validity.

VALIDITY OF THE HCSBS   6

According to the *Standards for Educational and Psychological Testing* (AERA, APA, & NCME, 1999), *test validity* is "the degree to which evidence and theory support the interpretations of test scores entailed by proposed uses of tests" (p. 9). In other words, validity reflects how effective a test is for its purported purposes. Validity is considered to be the most important issue in developing and evaluating tests (Gregory, 2000; Salvia & Ysseldyke, 2000). It is important to consider that *test validation is a process rather than a single product*. No single set of research data or other evidence proves with absolute certainty that a test is valid. Rather, each piece of validity evidence that accumulates strengthens or weakens the claims of validity for an assessment tool.

The *Standards* considers that validity is a unitary concept: "It is the degree to which all the accumulated evidence supports the intended interpretation of test scores for the proposed purpose" (p. 11). The discussion of validity in the *Standards* emphasizes types of validity evidence rather than specific types of validity and does not follow traditional psychometric terminology, such as construct validity, content validity, and so forth. Instead, the *Standards* details differing ways that validity evidence is accumulated. The discussion of validity evidence for the HCSBS that is presented in this chapter follows this pattern of presenting evidence based on the differing ways that the *Standards* maintains validity evidence is accumulated. For the sake of continuity with longstanding traditional terminology used by psychometric experts and test users in discussing validity, the traditional terms are also used where they are appropriate.

EVIDENCE BASED ON TEST CONTENT

The *Standards* states, "Important validity evidence can be obtained from an analysis of the relationship between a test's content and the construct it is intended to measure" (p. 11). In traditional psychometric terminology, this type of validity evidence is referred to as *content validity*. This type of validity evidence requires careful examination and judgment of a test to determine how relevant its contents are to the construct that is intended to be measured (Cronbach, 1990; Gregory, 2000; Salvia & Ysseldyke, 2000). For the HCSBS, this process should involve an accumulation of information regarding how well the item contents of the scale reflect the constructs of social competence and antisocial behavior.

As described in Chapter 4, the development of the HCSBS was based on the item content and rating format of the original SSBS, its school-based cross-informant counterpart. Chapter 4 describes in detail the great care that was taken to develop the initial item pool for the SSBS to represent the constructs of social competence and antisocial behavior of children and youth in school settings. These items were carefully reworded for the HCSBS to reflect social competence and antisocial behavior within home and community contexts. The item development procedures included a review of the literature and existing measures and intervention programs, item refinement and reduction to eliminate redundancy, and content validation using expert judges. For both instruments, the Social Competence scale was designed to reflect the most important forms of social adjustment: peer related, teacher or adult related, and self-related. The Antisocial Behavior scales of both measures were carefully crafted to reflect both covert and overt forms of antisocial behavior. Because of these carefully enacted and theory-driven development procedures, the HCSBS has solid evidence of *face validity*, an important initial type of content validity.

Although evidence that supports the presumption of face validity is an important first step, there are additional data-driven procedures to help determine whether the contents of a test reflect accurately the construct that is purported to be measured. Educational assessment experts Salvia and Ysseldyke (2000) suggested that individual test items that do not correlate at least moderately well (.25–.30 or more) with the total score of a test (and by inference, with any subscale scores to which they are connected) probably do not belong in the same domain that is being assessed by the scale. To assess the content validity of the HCSBS in this manner, bivariate product-moment correlations between individual items and their respective total scores (Social Competence Total or Antisocial Behavior Total) and subscale scores were computed using individual item data from the entire norming sample of 1,562 cases.

For both the item-subscale and item-total correlations, this procedure produced associations well in excess of the recommended minimum levels and indicate that the items grouped together in each scale and subscale are relatively homogenous and belong to the same general domain. The item-total correlations for the Social Competence Scale range from .62 to .79, and the item-subscale correlations for this scale range from .65 to .84. The item-total correlations for the Antisocial Behavior scale range from .61 to .81, and the item-subscale correlations range from .58 to .81. The coefficients from these analyses for each of the 64 items of the HCSBS are presented by subscale domains in Table 6.1 (for the Social Competence scale) and Table 6.2 (for the Antisocial Behavior scale).

Overall, the procedures used to develop the contents of the HCSBS items were done carefully and in a theory-driven manner, resulting in the constructs of social competence and antisocial behavior of children and youth in home and community contexts being well represented in the rating items of the two major scales. In addition, the item-total correlation procedure provides strong

Table 6.1. Item-subscale correlations, item-total correlations, and factor loading values for HCSBS Social Competence scale

HCSBS items, by subscale	Item-subscale	Item-total	Factor load
Peer Relations			
1. Cooperates with peers	.72	.72	.76
4. Offers help to peers when needed	.71	.69	.68
5. Participates effectively in family or group activities	.65	.65	.67
6. Understands problems and needs of peers	.76	.74	.76
9. Invites peers to participate in activities	.71	.62	.69
11. Has skills or abilities that are admired by peers	.74	.72	.74
12. Is accepting of peers	.77	.74	.77
15. Will give in or compromise with peers when appropriate	.66	.68	.66
19. Interacts with a wide variety of peers	.75	.68	.78
21. Is good at initiating or joining conversations with peers	.76	.67	.76
22. Is sensitive to the feelings of others	.71	.71	.67
25. Enters appropriately into ongoing activities with peers	.81	.76	.83
26. Has good leadership skills	.76	.72	.76
28. Notices and compliments accomplishments of others	.74	.72	.72
29. Is assertive in an appropriate way when he or she needs to be	.71	.67	.71
30. Is invited by peers to join in activities	.74	.68	.78
32. Is "looked up to" or respected by peers	.79	.76	.82
Self-Management/Compliance			
2. Makes appropriate transitions between different activities	.67	.69	.67
3. Completes chores without being reminded	.71	.62	.74
7. Remains calm when problems arise	.71	.66	.71
8. Listens to and carries out directions from parents or supervisors	.79	.72	.83
10. Asks appropriately for clarification of instructions	.71	.71	.71
13. Completes chores or other assigned tasks independently	.74	.65	.82
14. Completes chores or other assigned tasks on time	.76	.67	.81
16. Follows family and community rules	.84	.74	.82
17. Behaves appropriately at school	.82	.77	.81
18. Asks for help in an appropriate manner	.77	.75	.75
20. Produces work of acceptable quality for his or her ability level	.69	.68	.67
23. Responds appropriately when corrected by parents or supervisors	.76	.72	.81
24. Controls temper when angry	.75	.72	.77
27. Adjusts to different behavioral expectations across settings	.77	.79	.76
31. Shows self-control	.79	.76	.81

Note: All correlations are significant at $p < .001$.

evidence to bolster the argument that the items within each of the two HCSBS major scales are strongly linked to the overall constructs measured by those scales. In sum, there appears to be strong evidence for the validity of the HCSBS based on the specific contents of the test and how those contents were developed.

Table 6.2. Item-subscale correlations, item-total correlations, and factor loading values for HCSBS Antisocial Behavior scale

HCSBS items, by subscale	Item-subscale	Item-total	Factor load
Defiant/Disruptive			
1. Blames others for his or her problems	.66	.62	.66
3. Is defiant to parents or supervisors	.75	.72	.81
6. Is dishonest; tells lies	.68	.69	.71
8. Is disrespectful or "sassy"	.72	.69	.78
9. Is easily provoked; has a "short fuse"	.79	.76	.85
10. Ignores parents or supervisors	.78	.76	.83
14. Has temper outbursts or tantrums	.78	.75	.84
16. Is overly demanding of attention from adults	.72	.77	.74
21. Whines and complains	.73	.68	.73
23. Is difficult to control	.79	.81	.88
24. Bothers and annoys others	.76	.77	.81
28. Is not dependable	.69	.67	.71
30. Acts impulsively without thinking	.77	.74	.79
31. Is easily irritated	.78	.73	.84
32. Demands help from peers	.61	.62	.56
Antisocial/Aggressive			
2. Takes things that are not his or hers	.64	.63	.66
4. Cheats on schoolwork or in games	.64	.61	.62
5. Gets into fights	.71	.67	.76
7. Teases and makes fun of others	.66	.62	.75
11. Acts as if he or she is better than others	.65	.61	.61
12. Destroys or damages others' property	.74	.69	.77
13. Will not share with others	.63	.62	.63
15. Disregards feelings or needs of others	.77	.77	.77
17. Threatens others; is verbally aggressive	.81	.76	.83
18. Swears or uses offensive language	.65	.61	.71
19. Is physically aggressive	.75	.71	.79
20. Insults peers	.58	.68	.82
22. Argues or quarrels with peers	.73	.74	.77
25. Gets into trouble at school or in the community	.75	.73	.75
26. Disrupts ongoing activities	.74	.73	.76
27. Boasts and brags	.63	.61	.66
29. Is cruel to other persons or to animals	.77	.72	.82

Note: All correlations are significant at $p < .001$.

EVIDENCE BASED ON INTERNAL STRUCTURE

The *Standards* states, "Analyses of the internal structure of a test can indicate the degree to which the relationships among test items and test components conform to the construct on which the proposed test score interpretations are based" (p. 13). The type of validity evidence that this statement describes has traditionally been referred to in general terms as *construct validity*, or evidence that the test is indeed measuring the hypothesized theoretical construct(s) that it is designed to measure. One of the specific ways that validity has been determined in this manner is through factor analytic studies to evaluate the underlying structure of the instrument, which has been referred to as *factorial validity* (Gregory, 2000; Salvia & Ysseldyke,

2000). A related way that validity evidence is evaluated is through an examination of the intercorrelations among scales and subscales of a measure. Results of both types of validity procedures are presented in this section.

Factor Structure

Exploratory and higher-order factor analytic procedures were conducted with the HCSBS items (see Table 6.3). These analyses, from a study by Merrell and Crowley (2000), resulted in the development of the two-subscale structure for both the Social Competence and Antisocial Behavior scales.

Methods Analyses were conducted using the initial large wave of data from the national standardization sample, from which the final norming samples were drawn. This sample included ratings of 2,024 children and youth ranging in age from 5 to 18 years old. This sample was approximately 53% boys and 47% girls.

The primary analysis strategy was exploratory factor analysis. Gorsuch (1997) criticized what he referred to as the *little jiffy* solution in factor analysis. By this term, he meant the default options on most statistical packages, which are usually principal components analysis with a varimax rotation. Based on Gorsuch's recommendations, the authors of HCSBS used common factor analysis and an oblique (promax) rotation. Consequently, a higher-order factor analysis (factoring of the factors, rather than the items) was conducted.

To assess for invariance in the factor structure, the sample was randomly split in half, and initial analyses were conducted on half of the sample (n = 1,030). The second half of the sample was used to test for the replicability of the factors (n = 994). In general, items were quite consistent in their loading in each half of the sample; however, a handful (approximately 5) items changed factors with the replication. To address this issue, two strategies were used: Additional random splits of the data were used to see where the item loaded most frequently, and the theoretical literature related to social skills was considered to determine where the item would best fit.

Table 6.3. Results of higher-order factor analysis

HCSBS scales	Loading on higher-order factor
Social Competence	
Peer Relations	.90
Self-Management/Compliance	.90
Antisocial Behavior	
Defiant/Disruptive	.93
Antisocial/Aggressive	.93

Because the theoretical foundation on which the HCSBS rests is predicated on the constructs of social competence and antisocial behavior being associated but independent, analyses were conducted for each scale separately. The same analytic strategy, however, was applied in each instance. The results discussed are those for the first split of the sample ($n = 1,030$), as the second half of the sample was used merely for replication.

Results: Social Competence Scale The recommended solution identified for the Social Competence scale was a two-factor solution, accounting for 58.6% of the variance. Factor 1, which was titled *Peer Relations*, consisted of 17 items focusing on the child's relationships with his or her peers (e.g., *Is accepting of peers, Interacts with a wide variety of peers*). Factor 2, which was titled *Self-Management/Compliance*, consisted of 15 items including *Shows self-control, Behaves appropriately at school*, and *Completes chores or assigned tasks on time*. The correlation between the two factors was quite high ($r = .77$). It is important to note that the factor loadings for all items were quite high on both factors, suggesting a strong higher-order factor. Thus, in interpretation, the highest loading for each item was considered to identify the factor placement. Factor loadings for the items of the Social Competence scale are presented by subscale in Table 6.1.

A higher-order factor analysis was conducted using the first-level factor correlation matrix. One factor was extracted, on which both primary factors loaded highly ($r = .90$ for both factors). The higher-order factor accounted for 80.7% of the variance in the primary factors and can be interpretively considered as the broad construct of social competence.

Replication of the Social Competence scale indicated that the factor loadings were fairly stable at the primary level. Two items showed some movement during the second analysis. The higher-order factor was quite stable in all analyses. As previously noted, items tended to load highly on both primary factors, indicating that the Social Competence scale is best considered as a unitary scale. For clinical and research purposes, however, the two subscales identified may be helpful to better understand the relative strengths of a given child or to better investigate specific aspects of social competence.

Results: Antisocial Behavior Scale The recommended solution identified for the Antisocial Behavior scale was also a two-factor solution, accounting for 58.5% of the variance. Factor 1, titled *Defiant/Disruptive*, consisted of 15 items focusing on the tendency to flaunt authority and be difficult in a variety of situations (e.g., *Is disrespectful or "sassy," Is difficult to control, Whines and complains*). Factor 2, titled *Antisocial/Aggressive*, consisted of 17 items reflecting overt and covert antisocial behaviors and aggressive conduct problems, including *Threatens others; is verbally aggressive, Takes things that are not his or hers*, and *Is cruel to other persons or to animals*. The correlation between the factors was again quite high ($r = .82$). Similarly to the Social Competence scale, the factor loadings for all items were quite high on both factors and the highest loading for each item was considered to identify the factor placement. Factor loadings for items in the Antisocial Behavior scale are presented by subscale in Table 6.2.

A higher-order factor analysis was conducted using the first-level factor correlation matrix. One factor was extracted, on which both primary factors loaded highly ($r = .93$ for both factors). The higher-order factor accounted for 86.5% of the variance in the primary factors and can be interpretively considered as representing the broad construct of antisocial behavior.

Replication of the Antisocial Behavior scale indicated that the factor loadings were fairly stable at the primary level, with only three items showing movement during the replication. The higher-order factor was quite stable in all analyses. As previously noted, items tended to load highly on both primary factors, indicating that this scale is best considered as a unitary scale; however, the two subscales identified may provide more specific information for clinical and research purposes.

Conclusions The identified two-factor structures for each of the HCSBS major scales are consistent with current theory and research on social competence and antisocial behavior and shed some additional light on this area. The subscale structure that was developed through these factor analytic procedures is quite congruent with the theoretical foundation on which the instrument was built. Although there are some differences in the subscale structures of the HCSBS in comparison with its cross-setting counterpart, the SSBS-2, such contrasts based on differing samples and contexts are not unusual, and there is still a good deal of similarity in how the items tend to cluster together. It is also important to consider that the higher-order (one-factor) solutions were more psychometrically sound. Thus, as is indicated in Chapter 3, the total scores for each of the two scales should be considered the most important indicator for interpretation of scores; however, the subscale scores may be an interesting supplement for clinical interpretation and additional research, or in some cases, as an adjunct to the total scores for clinical interpretation.

The utility of the identified factors or subscales is directly dependent on their psychometric characteristics. In this regard, the reliability and SEM tables in Chapter 5 indicate without exception that the psychometric properties of the HCSBS subscales developed through these factor analytic procedures are very strong. In all cases, the internal consistency of the scales is quite high, surpassing .90. The reliability indicators for the HCSBS subscales provide additional support for their use.

In sum, the results of the factor analytic procedures conducted for the HCSBS bolster the validity of the measure. The obtained factor or subscale clusters reflect clinically relevant constructs that are consistent with current theory, and the broader constructs of social competence and antisocial behavior appear to be the superordinate or higher-order constructs.

Intercorrelations Among HCSBS Scale Scores

The *Standards* discusses the notion of validity evidence based on the internal structure of a test, stating

The conceptual framework for a test may imply a single dimension of behavior, or it may posit several components that are each expected to be homogeneous, but that are also distinct from each other...the extent to which item interrelationships bear out the presumptions of the framework would be relevant to validity. (AERA, APA, & NCME, 1999, p. 13)

One of the primary traditional ways that the internal structure of a test is examined in this manner is to develop a matrix of correlations among identified subscale and total scores and to explore the direction and strength of these relationships to determine how consistent they are with theory regarding the constructs purported to be measured. Therefore, in addition to the factor analytic data, the internal structure of the HCSBS was explored through analyses of within-scale relationships in this manner.

Table 6.4 presents a matrix of intercorrelations among HCSBS subscale and total scores, based on bivariate Pearson product-moment correlations among all score variables for the entire norming sample of 1,562 cases. In general, these correlations indicate that the scales of the HCSBS are highly interrelated, particularly within each of the two major scales, Social Competence and Antisocial Behavior. The correlations between the Social Competence subscales and the Social Competence Total score range from .84 to .96, indicating that each subscale taps a construct that is highly related to the higher-order construct of social competence.

A similar pattern holds true for the interrelationships of HCSBS scores in the Antisocial Behavior scale, where the correlations between the two subscales and the Antisocial Behavior Total score range from .89 to .97 and indicate that each subscale taps a construct that is highly related to the overall construct of antisocial behavior. Although the factor analytic research provides convincing evidence regarding the unique aspects of the two identified subscales for each of the two major scales, it is important to not place too much weight on subscale scores but to consider the total scores for each scale as the most important indicators of social behavior.

The pattern of correlations between the Social Competence and Antisocial Behavior scores is interesting and is more complex than the pattern of correlations within each scale. It has been proposed by the senior author of the HCSBS that the constructs of social competence and antisocial behavior

Table 6.4. Intercorrelations among HCSBS subscale and total scores

HCSBS scales	PR	SMC	SCT	DD	AA	ABT
Peer Relations (PR)	1.00					
Self-Management/Compliance (SMC)	.84	1.00				
Social Competence Total (SCT)	.96	.96	1.00			
Defiant/Disruptive (DD)	−.68	−.82	−.78	1.00		
Antisocial/Aggressive (AA)	−.65	−.73	−.72	.89	1.00	
Antisocial Behavior Total (ABT)	−.68	−.80	−.77	.97	.97	1.00

Note: All correlations are significant at $p < .001$.

should be considered and measured separately, even though there is an obvious negative relationship between them (Merrell, 2008; Merrell & Gimpel, 1998). To this end, the HCSBS Social Competence and Antisocial Behavior scales were constructed separately, and the scores are derived separately. As is made clear by a close examination of the data in Table 6.4, the range of correlations between scores of the Social Competence and Antisocial Behavior scales is from –.65 to –.82, with a mean intercorrelation of –.74. Although the strength of association indicated by these coefficients is moderately strong, it is not as strong as the intercorrelations within each scale. The mean intercorrelation of –.74 between Social Competence and Antisocial Behavior scores, coupled with the correlation of –.77 between the total scores of the two scales, indicates that (by calculating r^2 values), on average, the two scales share approximately 54%–59% of their variance. This pattern of relationships is fairly substantial but still indicates that the two scales have about as much separate variance as shared variance. Therefore, these data indicate that HCSBS score interpretation should follow the proposed uses of the two scales. Although social competence and antisocial behavior share a moderately strong negative relationship, they are not merely polar opposites. Rather, each construct should be assessed separately rather than inferred from an examination of the other.

EVIDENCE BASED ON RELATIONS TO OTHER VARIABLES

The *Standards* states, "Analyses of the relationship of test scores to variables external to the test provide another important source of validity evidence" (p. 13). One type of analysis of this sort is examination of relationships between scores of a test and scores from other tests that have been designed to measure similar as well as differing constructs. "Relationships between test scores and other measures intended to assess similar constructs provide *convergent evidence*, whereas relationships between test scores and measures purportedly of different constructs provide *discriminant evidence*" (p. 14; italics added for emphasis). Convergent evidence has been traditionally referred to as *convergent construct validity*, whereas discriminant evidence has been referred to as *discriminant construct validity* (Gregory, 2000; Salvia & Ysseldyke, 2000).

During the development and standardization of the HCSBS, studies were conducted wherein scores of the HCSBS were compared with scores from eight other behavior rating scales or parent report instruments obtained from the same samples. The results of these studies are reviewed in this section. The results of the first five studies reviewed in this section have been previously published by the authors of the HCSBS and colleagues (Merrell, Caldarella, Streeter, Boelter, & Gentry, 2001). The sixth study in this section was part of a published study by Merrell and Boelter (2001). The final two studies in this section are from scientific papers presented at professional meetings by Dillon, Michael, and Huelsman (2001) and Michael, Dillon, and Huelsman (2001).

HCSBS and Social Skills Rating System

Scores of the HCSBS were compared with scores from the Social Skills Rating System (SSRS; Gresham & Elliott, 1990), with a sample of parent ratings of 59 students who were recruited from a public middle school in an urban area in the North Central region of the United States. The sample of students who were rated were all in the sixth grade and ranged in age from 11 to 13. Of the total sample of 59, there were 34 boys and 25 girls; 8 students were identified as having a learning disability. The sample was predominantly White (94%). Parent raters were asked to complete the demographic information sheet for the HCSBS norming sample and to rate their children using both the HCSBS and SSRS.

The SSRS is a norm-referenced, nationally standardized cross-informant rating scale system designed for screening children and youth suspected of having social behavior problems. It is one of the more widely used social skills rating scales currently available and is an excellent comparison instrument for evaluating the convergent construct validity of the HCSBS. The SSRS was developed to broadly assess social skills and sample the domains of academic competence and problem behavior. The parent rating form, which was used in this study, includes 55 items on four social skills subscales (Cooperation, Assertion, Self-Control, Responsibility) and a brief problem behavior screening scale. Reliability and validity evidence found in the SSRS test manual and in several external studies has been characterized in several reviews as adequate to excellent.

HCSBS and SSRS scores for this sample were compared by computing bivariate Pearson product-moment correlations across each set of scores for the two measures. The resulting correlation matrix is presented in Table 6.5. The coefficients in this table indicate associations between scores of the two measures in the expected direction and magnitude. The Social Competence Total score of the HCSBS and the SSRS Social Skills Total score are correlated at the .72 level, a moderately high association, indicating they are measuring

Table 6.5. Correlations between scores on the HCSBS and scores on the Social Skills Rating System (SSRS), Parent Rating Form, for parent ratings of 59 children ages 11–13

SSRS scales	HCSBS Scales					
	PR	SMC	SCT	DD	AA	ABT
Cooperation	.53	.49	.55	−.56	−.49	−.55
Assertion	.61	.33	.52	−.43	−.44	−.45
Responsibility	.48	.42	.48	−.42	−.55	−.51
Social Skills Total	.72	.62	.72	−.69	−.70	−.77
Externalizing Problems	−.56	−.50	−.57	.76	.72	.77
Internalizing Problems	−.65	−.45	−.60	.61	.50	.59
Hyperactivity	−.57	−.68	−.67	.78	.66	.75
Problem Behavior Total	−.70	−.62	−.71	.81	.72	.80

Note: All correlations are significant at $p < .01$.
Key: AA, Antisocial/Aggressive; ABT, Antisocial Behavior Total; DD, Defiant/Disruptive; PR, Peer Relations; SCT, Social Competence Total; SMC, Self-Management/Compliance.

similar constructs. Likewise, the HCSBS Antisocial Behavior Total scale and the SSRS Problem Behavior Total are correlated at .80. The Internalizing Problems score of the SSRS is associated with the HCSBS Antisocial Behavior scale scores at a somewhat lower level (ranging from .50 to .61), which is expected. The correlations between the two HCSBS Social Competence subscales and the three SSRS Social Skills subscales are smaller than the association between the total scores, ranging from .33 to .61, and indicating that the subscale structure of the two measures differs somewhat. Finally, the associations between positive social behavior and problem behavior scales across the two measures are negative as would be expected and moderate to moderately strong, ranging from –.42 to –.77.

In summary, the correlations between the HCSBS and SSRS provide support for the convergent and discriminant construct validity of both instruments. Scales that would be expected to measure similar constructs are correlated at a relatively high level, scales expected to measure opposing constructs are correlated negatively at a moderate to moderately high level, and scales measuring constructs expected to differ somewhat are correlated at a modest level.

HCSBS and Conners Parent Rating Scale, Revised

Scores from HCSBS ratings of 68 adolescents ages 12–14 (27 boys, 41 girls) were compared with their scores from the Conners Parent Rating Scale–Revised–Short Form (CPRS-R-S; Conners, 1997) using a sample of parent ratings from the same public middle school population that was used for the HCSBS–SSRS comparison study. Of the 68 students in the sample, 64 were general education students and 4 received special services because of learning disabilities. As was the case for the previous study, the sample was primarily White (94%) and from an urban area in the upper Midwest region. The same data collection procedures described for the previous study were also used in this study.

The CPRS-R-S is one component of the comprehensive Conners Rating System, Revised. This system contains teacher, parent, and student rater forms. It is an updated version of the original Conners Rating Scales and overlaps a great deal with items contained on the original scales. For the revised scales, however, some items were added or deleted to more specifically focus on attention-deficit/hyperactivity disorder (ADHD)–related behaviors, as outlined in DSM-IV (American Psychiatric Association, 1994) diagnostic criteria. The CPRS-R-S is a 27-item parent rating instrument designed for assessment of children and adolescents ages 3–17. It contains four subscales—Oppositional, Cognitive Problems, Hyperactivity, and ADHD Index—all of which focus on externalizing behaviors. The original CPRS underwent redevelopment and extensive restandardization, resulting in a revised parent rating scale with better psychometric properties than previous versions. Norms were derived from a large, representative sample of children in the United States and Canada. Psychometric data on the CPRS-R-S that are found in the test manual indicate that the technical properties of the CPRS-RS are adequate to excellent, as evidenced by strong internal reliability coefficients, high test–retest reliability, and various studies supporting the validity of these scales.

Bivariate Pearson product-moment correlations between the HCSBS and CPRS-R-S ratings from this sample are presented in Table 6.6. These correlations are all significant at the $p < .001$ level. Correlations between the HCSBS Social Competence scales and the four CPRS-R-S scales were negative, as expected, and moderate to moderately strong in magnitude, ranging from –.37 to –.81. Correlations between the HCSBS Antisocial Behavior scales and the four CPRS-R-S scales were positive and quite strong in magnitude, ranging from .61 to .89. These associations between scores of the two instruments indicate that the construct of social competence, as measured by the HCSBS, is negatively associated to a moderate level with the externalizing problem scores represented by the CPRS-R-S and that the construct of antisocial behavior, as measured by the HCSBS, is tapping a very similar construct to what is measured by the CPRS-R-S, with a median correlation of .76. Given what is known regarding the strong comorbid relationship between ADHD symptoms, social competence deficits, and antisocial behavior problems (e.g., Whalen & Henker, 1998) this relationship is not surprising and further supports the validity of the HCSBS as a measure of clinically relevant social and antisocial behavior.

HCSBS and Child Behavior Checklist

The HCSBS was compared with the Child Behavior Checklist (CBCL; Achenbach, 1991) using ratings from 60 parents of children ages 7–11 from an elementary school in a rural community in the Pacific Northwest region of the United States. The sample included 32 boys and 28 girls, with mean age of 9.7 years. These children were primarily Caucasian (85%) and in general education classrooms. The parent raters who agreed to participate were sent a research packet containing a consent form, an information and instruction letter, and the two behavior rating scales. Parents returned the completed research packets to researchers through the mail.

Table 6.6. Correlations between scores on the HCSBS and scores on the Conners Parent Rating Scale-Revised-Short Form (CPRS-R-S) for parent ratings of 68 adolescents ages 12-14

CPRS-R-S scales	HCSBS scales					
	PR	SMC	SCT	DD	AA	ABT
Oppositional	–.57	–.74	–.69	.89	.76	.87
Cognitive Problems	–.49	–.74	–.64	.77	.55	.69
Hyperactivity	–.37	–.63	–.52	.70	.68	.71
ADHD Index	–.64	–.81	–.77	.81	.61	.75

Note: All correlations are significant at $p < .001$.
Key: AA, Antisocial/Aggressive; ABT, Antisocial Behavior Total; DD, Defiant/Disruptive; PR, Peer Relations; SCT, Social Competence Total; SMC, Self-Management/Compliance.

The CBCL is a parent report form that covers a wide range of behavior and emotional problems. This instrument includes eight narrow-band subscales, two broad-band scales, and a total problems score, which is the sum of all problem items. The Externalizing Problems area includes the Aggressive Behavior and Delinquent Behavior narrow-band scales, whereas the Internalizing Problems area is composed of the Withdrawn, Somatic Complaints, and Anxiety/Depression narrow-band scales. In addition, there are three "mixed" syndrome narrow-band scales, Attention Problems, Social Problems, and Thought Problems. This nationally standardized norm-referenced instrument is used worldwide in clinical work and research with children and youth as part of the Achenbach System of Empirically-Based Assessment (ASEBA) and is the most widely researched child behavior rating scale currently available (Merrell, 2008). Extensive research has documented the strong psychometric properties of the CBCL, and it is viewed as one of the most reliable and valid behavior rating scales available for assessing clinically relevant problem behaviors of children and youth.

Bivariate Pearson product-moment correlations between the HCSBS scale scores and the various CBCL scale scores are presented in Table 6.7. For the HCSBS Social Competence Total score, the range of correlations with the CBCL problem scales is $-.18$ to $-.67$, with a mean correlation of $-.50$ across the 11 CBCL scores. The insignificant correlation of $-.18$ with the CBCL Social Problems narrow-band scale is surprisingly low; however, the face similarity in constructs is deceiving. A closer look at the items in the Social Problems scale reveals little conceptual similarity (or polar dissimilarity) with the construct of social competence as measured by the HCSBS Social Competence scale. By contrast, the correlation of $-.67$ between the HCSBS Social Competence Total score and the CBCL Total Problems score is moderately large and in the expected range and direction. The Social Competence subscales follow the same general patterns as the total score in their associations with the CBCL problem behavior scores.

Table 6.7. Correlations between scores on the HCSBS and scores on the Child Behavior Checklist (CBCL) for parent ratings of 60 children ages 7–11

CBCL scales	HCSBS scales					
	PR	SMC	SCT	DD	AA	ABT
Aggressive Behavior	−.48**	−.47**	−.50**	.50**	.40**	.48**
Anxiety/Depression	−.29*	−.24*	−.28*	.31*	.21	.28*
Attention Problems	−.50**	−.49**	−.52**	.54**	.39*	.50**
Delinquent Behavior	−.43**	−.40**	−.44**	.31*	.32*	.34*
Social Problems	−.17	−.15	−.18	.17	.20	.20
Thought Problems	−.43**	−.38**	−.43**	.46**	.42**	.47
Withdrawn	−.60**	−.61**	−.64**	.68**	.72**	.73**
Externalizing Problems Total	−.58**	−.48**	−.64**	.76**	.74**	.79**
Internalizing Problems Total	−.52**	−.48**	−.52**	.55**	.41**	.52**
Total Problems	−.63**	−.65**	−.67**	.70**	.61**	.70**

Key: *p < .01; **p < .001; AA, Antisocial/Aggressive; ABT, Antisocial Behavior Total; DD, Defiant/Disruptive; PR, Peer Relations; SCT, Social Competence Total; SMC, Self-Management/Compliance.

For the HCSBS Antisocial Behavior Total score, the range of correlations with the various CBCL problem scales was .20 to .79, with a mean correlation of .51. The two Antisocial Behavior subscales have a generally similar range of correlations with the CBCL scores. The wide range of correlations indicates a wide range of similarity across constructs measured by the two scales. As would be expected, the Antisocial Behavior scale evidenced the strongest correlations with conceptually similar scales on the CBCL: the highest correlation between the two was .79 between the Antisocial Behavior Total and the CBCL Externalizing Problems Total, indicating that the two scales are tapping similar constructs. The insignificant correlation of .20 between the Antisocial Behavior Total score and the CBCL Social Problems score is also surprisingly low when one considers the similarity in titles between the two scales. Again, the answer to this unexpected finding is that the content of the Social Problems scale is quite dissimilar to the content of the overall construct of antisocial behavior. Items such as *Acts too young for his/her age, Clings to adults or is too dependent, Gets teased a lot, Poorly coordinated or clumsy,* and *Prefers playing with younger children* appear to have more in common with the construct of emotional immaturity than the construct of antisocial behavior and are more in contrast to this construct than to the general construct of social competence. The internalizing problems scores of the CBCL tend to be weakly to moderately correlated with the HCSBS Antisocial Behavior scores, an expected finding.

HCSBS and Behavioral Assessment System for Children

Scores from the HCSBS were compared with scores from the parent rating scales of the Behavioral Assessment System for Children (BASC-PRS; Reynolds & Kamphaus, 1992) using data from a large clinical sample. The raters in this sample were parents or guardians of 206 children and adolescents who were receiving inpatient treatment for severe behavior and emotional problems at a large hospital in an urban center of the Northeastern United States. There were two separate groups within this general sample, based on child age range: a child sample that included ratings of 76 children ranging in age from 6 to 11 and an adolescent sample that included ratings of 130 youth ranging in age from 12 to 18. The 206 children and youth in this sample were predominately Caucasian (90%) and male (74%).

Research packets containing the HCSBS, the age-appropriate parent rating scale form of the BASC, and a sheet requesting demographic information regarding the child and rater were given to parents or guardians of children and adolescents in the inpatient treatment program. The participants completed the research packets as part of the initial admission assessment for their children. The completed rating forms included all of the youth who were admitted to the treatment program over a span of approximately 6 months.

The BASC parent rating scales are one component of a multidimensional, multimethod system for assessment and identification of school-age children with emotional disturbances and behavior disorders. The BASC-PRS is available in three forms: preschool (ages 4–5), child (ages 6–11), and adolescent (ages 12–18). The child and adolescent age range forms were used in this study. The BASC-PRS is a nationally standardized, norm-referenced, comprehensive measure of adaptive and problem behaviors. These instruments include 126–148 items (depending on the age range version) that are rated using a three-point rating form. Behaviors are classified along the following dimensions: Hyperactivity, Aggression, Conduct Problems, Anxiety, Depression, Somatization, Atypicality, Withdrawal, Attention Problems, Adaptability [child form only], Social Skills, and Leadership. These scales are grouped according to the clinical composites of Externalizing Problems (Hyperactivity, Aggression, and Conduct Problems), Internalizing Problems (Anxiety, Depression, and Somatization), and Adaptive Skills (Leadership and Social Skills). The Behavioral Symptoms Index is composed of the Aggression, Hyperactivity, Anxiety, Depression, and Atypicality scales. Based on extensive evidence presented in the BASC examiner's manual and in subsequent published studies, psychometric properties of the BASC-PRS are considered to be adequate to excellent, and the BASC is considered to be a model rating scale assessment system (Merrell, 2008).

Bivariate Pearson product-moment correlations between the HCSBS and BASC-PRS scores for the inpatient child group are presented in Table 6.8, and correlations between the HCSBS and BASC-PRS scores for the inpatient adolescent group are presented in Table 6.9. The pattern of correlations between the HCSBS and BASC-PRS is remarkably similar across the two age range forms. Because the BASC has such a large number of specific scales and there are so many correlations in this matrix, it is most useful to consider the patterns of correlation between measures based on sets of similar scales.

Table 6.8. Correlations between scores on the HCSBS and the Behavior Assessment System for Children, Parent Rating Scale, Child Version (BASC-PRS-C), for parent ratings of 76 children ages 6–11

BASC-PRS-C scales	HCSBS scales					
	PR	SMC	SCT	DD	AA	ABT
Hyperactivity	−.40**	−.52**	−.47**	.63**	.49**	.58**
Aggression	−.57**	−.61**	−.61**	.78**	.86**	.87**
Conduct Problems	−.46**	−.44**	−.47**	.55**	.66**	.65**
Anxiety	.09	.07	.09	.09	.07	.10
Depression	−.35**	−.40**	−.39*	.51**	.43**	.49**
Somatization	−.08	−.01	−.05	.02	.08	.07
Atypicality	−.14	−.20	−.16	.26*	.18	.24*
Withdrawal	−.31**	−.24*	−.28*	.13	.09	.12
Attention Problems	−.47**	−.54**	−.52**	.53**	.35**	.46**
Adaptability	.52	.56**	.57**	−.52**	−.43**	−.49**
Social Skills	.72**	.69**	.74**	−.57**	−.53**	−.57**
Leadership	.63**	.52**	.59**	−.36**	−.31*	−.35**
EP Composite	−.55**	−.62**	−.61**	.78**	.79**	.83**
IP Composite	−.18	−.18	−.20	.33**	.29*	.33**
BSI Composite	−.40**	−.49**	−.46**	.63**	.54**	.62**
AS Composite	.76**	.73**	.78**	−.59**	−.53**	−.58**

Key: *p < .01; **p < .001; AA, Antisocial/Aggressive; ABT, Antisocial Behavior Total; AS, Adaptive Skills; BSI, Behavior Symptoms Index; DD, Defiant/Disruptive; EP, Externalizing Problems; IP, Internalizing Problems; PR, Peer Relations; SCT, Social Competence Total; SMC, Self-Management/Compliance.

Table 6.9. Correlations between scores on the HCSBS and scores on the Behavior Assessment System for Children, Parent Rating Scale, Adolescent Version (BASC-PRS-A), for parent ratings of 130 adolescents ages 12–18

BASC-PRS-A scales	HCSBS scales					
	PR	SMC	SCT	DD	AA	ABT
Hyperactivity	–.62**	–.72**	–.78**	.73**	.74**	.76**
Aggression	–.60**	–.70**	–.72**	.81**	.88*	.88**
Conduct Problems	–.49**	–.71**	–.69**	.73**	.74**	.76**
Anxiety	–.13	–.01	–.08	–.01	–.08	–.04
Depression	–.40**	.41**	–.44*	.49**	.40**	.46**
Somatization	–.02	.01	.02	.06	.08	-.07
Atypicality	–.31**	–.30**	–.32**	.36**	.38**	.38**
Withdrawal	–.26**	–.06	–.18*	.07	.08	.08
Attention Problems	–.48**	–.70**	–.63**	.60**	.53**	.59**
Social Skills	.73**	.71**	.77**	–.68	–.70**	–.71**
Leadership	.53**	.41**	.51**	–.27**	–.22*	–.25**
EP Composite	–.65**	–.82**	–.78**	.86**	.90**	.91**
IP Composite	–.23**	–.17*	–.22	.19*	.12	.16
BSI Composite	–.59**	–.66**	–.67**	.70**	.68**	.71**
AS Composite	.72**	.65**	.74**	–.57**	–.55**	–.58**

Key: *p < .01; **p < .001; AA, Antisocial/Aggressive; ABT, Antisocial Behavior Total; AS, Adaptive Skills; BSI, Behavior Symptoms Index; DD, Defiant/Disruptive; EP, Externalizing Problems; IP, Internalizing Problems; PR, Peer Relations; SCT, Social Competence Total; SMC, Self-Management/Compliance.

Correlations between the HCSBS Social Competence scale and the conceptually similar subscales from the BASC (Social Skills, Leadership, Adaptability [child form only], and Adaptive Skills Composite) were moderate to strong, ranging from .51 to .78 with the Social Competence Total scores across the child and adolescent versions. By contrast, correlations between the HCSBS Social Competence scale and the various disruptive behavior problems subscales of the BASC-PRS were negative and strong, generally in the –.60 to –.70 range and indicating the expected pattern of negative relationships between constructs. On the other hand, correlations between the HCSBS Social Competence scale and BASC subscales that had conceptually little relationship to social competence (e.g., Anxiety, Somatization, Withdrawal, Internalizing Composite) were weak, and in some cases near zero. These weak relationships provide discriminant evidence of the validity of the HCSBS Social Competence scale.

Regarding correlations between the HCSBS Antisocial Behavior scale and the BASC-PRS scales, the strongest relationships were evident in the case of the BASC disruptive behavior problem scales (Hyperactivity, Aggression, Conduct Problems, and Externalizing Composite), where the coefficients ranged from .58 to .91 with the Antisocial Behavior Total scores across the child and adolescent versions, depending on the specific scale and age range form, with a median value in the high .70s. These relationships provide solid evidence for the construct validity of the Antisocial Behavior scale. In contrast, the moderately strong negative relationships between the HCSBS Antisocial Behavior scale and the BASC-PRS Adaptability, Social Skills, and

VALIDITY OF THE HCSBS

Leadership scales provide additional support for the antisocial behavior construct. In addition, the weak (often near zero) relationships between the Antisocial Behavior scale and conceptually unrelated scales from the BASC-PRS, such as Anxiety, Somatization, Withdrawal, and Internalizing Composite provide discriminant evidence of the construct validity of the Antisocial Behavior scale.

HCSBS and ADHD Symptoms Rating Scale

Scores from the HCSBS were compared with scores from the ADHD Symptoms Rating Scale (ADHD-SRS; Holland, Gimpel, & Merrell, 2001) using ratings from parents of 148 middle school students ages 11–15 who rated their children using both measures. Participants in this study were from a medium-sized school district in a rural, small town community in the Southwestern United States who were recruited through letters sent from the principal of the school. Of the 148 parents who provided ratings, 129 were mothers of the students, and 19 were fathers. The gender distribution of the youth who were rated consisted of 66 boys (45%) and 82 girls (55%). In terms of ethnicity of the youth, 55% were White, 39% where Hispanic, and the remaining 6% where listed as either Native American or African American. Of the 148 students who were rated, 15 (10%) received special education services, whereas the remaining 90% did not have identified disabilities or receive special education services.

The ADHD-SRS is a 56-item behavior rating scale designed to assist in evaluating ADHD characteristics of school-age children. This scale may be completed by either teachers or parents, with separate norms available for each group. The 56 items were developed specifically based on the assessment criteria for ADHD from the DSM-IV. The empirically derived subscale structure of the ADHD-SRS for both the teacher and parent norms is very consistent with the two domains of ADHD symptoms from DSM-IV, and the subscales are thus labeled Inattention and Hyperactive-Impulsive. The standardization sample for this instrument is from a nationwide sample and includes more than 2,000 cases. Research evidence presented in the examiner's manual and in other published sources indicates that this instrument has adequate to excellent psychometric properties.

The resulting bivariate Pearson product-moment correlations for this study are presented in Table 6.10. Correlations between the HCSBS Social Competence scale and the ADHD-SRS scores were negative and ranged from −.41 to −.60, indicating that Social Competence scores are related to ADHD characteristics in a moderate and negative manner. With this sample, as ADHD symptoms increased, positive social characteristics were somewhat likely to decrease and vice versa. The correlations between the Antisocial Behavior scale and ADHD-SRS scores were positive and relatively strong, ranging from .69 to .77, indicating for this sample that as ADHD symptoms increased, so did ratings of antisocial behavior characteristics from the HCSBS.

Table 6.10. Correlations between scores on the HCSBS and scores on the ADHD Symptoms Rating Scale (ADHD-SRS) for parent ratings of 148 youth ages 11-15

HCSBS scales	ADHD-SRS scales		
	Hyperactive-Impulsive	Inattention	Total score
Peer Relations	−.41	−.48	−.45
Self-Management/Compliance	−.54	−.60	−.59
Social Competence Total	−.49	−.56	−.54
Defiant/Disruptive	.73	.70	.74
Antisocial/Aggressive	.75	.69	.75
Antisocial Behavior Total	.76	.73	.77

Note: All correlations are significant at $p < .01$.

This study provides evidence of the general relationship between the constructs of social/antisocial behavior and ADHD characteristics in a large sample of typical youth. Based on these results, it appears that although both forms of social behavior are moderately to strongly associated with ADHD characteristics, antisocial behavior is somewhat more strongly linked to this differing construct than prosocial behavior. In other words, if these findings were to replicate across situations, children with significant ADHD symptoms would be likely to evidence both deficits in social competence and excesses in antisocial behaviors, but the antisocial behavior excesses would likely be a somewhat stronger and more direct link to the ADHD symptoms than would be the social competence deficits.

These results provide additional evidence in support of the validity of the HCSBS and demonstrate a compelling link between social behavior and ADHD characteristics. The moderately strong negative relationship between Social Competence scores and the ADHD-SRS scores indicates that the presence of ADHD symptoms of inattention, impulsivity, and hyperactivity is likely to be accompanied by moderate deficits in social skills. The strong positive relationship between Antisocial Behavior scores and ADHD-SRS scores indicates a pattern of strong co-occurring relationships between these constructs, which is a well-documented phenomenon.

HCSBS and Psychopathy Screening Device

In an investigation of the predictive power of the constructs of social competence, callous-unemotional personality traits, and narcissistic personality traits, Dillon, Michael, and Huelsman (2001) evaluated self-report and parent report data for 66 adolescents who were incarcerated. These juvenile offenders ranged in age from 14 to 18 and were all male. Approximately 55% of the participants were Black, 40% were White, and 5% were Hispanic.

As part of this study, Social Competence Total scores from the HCSBS were correlated with scores from the parent report form of the Psychopathy Screening Device (PSD; Frick, Bodin, & Barry, 2000). The PSD is an experimental 20-item self- and observer report instrument that is purported to measure *psychopathic* traits of children and adolescents, which are defined as the antisocial characteristics of callousness, unemotionality, self-centeredness, and lack of regard for others. The PSD includes two subscales: Callous-Unemotional and Narcissism. The former subscale is thought to measure characteristics related to disregard of others' feelings and needs and lack of normal emotional arousal. The latter subscale is thought to measure characteristics related to self-centeredness.

Bivariate correlations between the HCSBS Social Competence Total score and the PSD scores were as follows: Callous-Unemotional, $-.59$, and Narcissism, $-.37$. These correlations were both statistically significant at the $p < .05$ level. The strength of these negative correlations could be characterized as moderate, and they indicate that with respect to parent perceptions of social-emotional characteristics of the target youth, social competence is negatively associated to a moderate degree with psychopathic personality traits.

In a related study using the same sample of 66 male juvenile offenders as the previous study, Michael, Dillon, and Huelsman (2001) explored the relationship between parenting practices, personality traits, and adolescent conduct problems. As part of this study, Antisocial Behavior Total scores of the HCSBS were correlated with scores from the parent report form of the PSD.

Bivariate correlations between the HCSBS Antisocial Behavior Total score and the two PSD subscales were as follows: Callous-Unemotional, .47, and Narcissism, .73. Both coefficients were significant at the $p < .05$ level. These results indicate a moderate to strong correlation between the constructs measured by the two instruments, which share roughly 22%–53% of their variance. Given that the construct of antisocial behavior as it is purported to be measured by the HCSBS is related (but not parallel) to the constructs purported to be measured by the PSD, these findings are in the expected direction.

Evidence of the convergent and discriminant construct validity of the HCSBS from these two studies are in the expected direction and of expected magnitude, given the constructs purported to be measured by the PSD. The fact that these studies specifically included youth who were incarcerated for violation of the law adds support to the use of the HCSBS with this population and allows inferences to be drawn beyond the scope of children and youth drawn from general school samples.

Summary of Convergent and Discriminant Validity Studies

In sum, the eight studies described in this section provide substantial evidence for the validity of the HCSBS as a measure of social competence and antisocial behavior. In general, correlations between Social Competence scores and other measures of social skills or adaptive social functioning from the comparison instruments were very strong and positive in direction. Correlations between Antisocial Behavior scores and various measures of externalizing conduct problems (including ADHD) were also very strong and positive in direction, evidencing strong similarity among these constructs.

Correlations between HCSBS scores and measures of personality that do not relate directly to social competence and antisocial behavior were more moderate in strength. Correlations between internalizing problems scores of the various comparison measures and both HCSBS scales were also modest in nature, correctly indicating that the constructs of social competence and antisocial behavior are only moderately related to internalizing problems such as depression, anxiety, and somatic problems. Finally, each of these six studies indicates a strong negative relationship between the constructs of social skills and externalizing problem behaviors. This last finding is consistent with the literature on the relationship between social skills and conduct problems, which indicates a strong negative relationship between these constructs but also calls for separate assessment of them, rather than inferring the presence or absence of one domain based on the presence or absence of the other (Merrell & Gimpel, 1998).

EVIDENCE BASED ON CONSEQUENCES OF TESTING

Another type of evidence that is relevant to the validity of the HCSBS involves analyses of expected group differences in scores. The *Standards* refers to this type of information as *evidence based on consequences of testing* and indicates that a test's demonstrated sensitivity to some examinee characteristic that is intended to be part of the test's construct provides evidence of its validity. In other words, if a test produces evidence of significant differences among groups where such evidence is an expected extension of the construct, then validity evidence is accumulated. If, however, a test shows evidence of significant group differences where none are anticipated or expected based on the construct purported to be measured, then the validity of the test may be questioned. Traditionally, this type of validation procedure—demonstration of a test's sensitivity to theoretically based group differences—has been included within the domain of *construct validity* (Gregory, 2000; Salvia & Ysseldyke, 2000).

This section includes evidence of theoretically consistent and expected group differences in HCSBS scores in several domains: at-risk identification status, special education classification status, clinical status, and gender. The results of these studies are summarized briefly in this section, providing enough evidence to document the validity of the HCSBS. For more specific details regarding these studies, refer to the original references.

Group Differences: At-Risk Status

One of the major purposes of the HCSBS is to identify children and youth who are at-risk for negative outcomes because of their deficits in social competence or their excesses in antisocial problem behavior. To help ascertain the validity of the instrument for this purpose, Merrell and Caldarella (1999) conducted a study to determine how efficiently parent ratings on this instrument would differentiate youth who evidenced social-behavioral risk characteristics from comparison youth who did not exhibit the risk characteristics. Parent ratings on the HCSBS were obtained on 267 children and adolescents in Grades 6–9 from an urban public school district in the Intermountain West region of the United States. Of the entire sample, 65.6% were male, 61.3% were Caucasian, and the age range was 11–16. The at-risk sample included 160 students who had been identified as "at-risk" by school personnel through a multiple-gating screening procedure designed to include seven domains of potential risk characteristics: academic performance, physical/behavioral symptoms, motivation, school/community involvement, social interaction patterns, family relations, and substance abuse behaviors. These students were identified as "at-risk" for the purposes of participating in a federally funded prevention project. A comparison group of 107 students was selected by referral from principals of the two schools participating in the prevention project, based on the absence of selection characteristics from the at-risk screening procedure. This comparison group was similar to the at-risk sample in terms of gender and ethnicity. Social Competence Total and Antisocial Behavior Total raw scores for the two groups were compared and contrasted, and the data were analyzed in a variety of ways to determine classification accuracy.

Descriptive statistics for HCSBS total raw scores of the two groups are presented in Table 6.11, along with analysis of variance procedure (ANOVA) results and ES estimates. The Social Competence Total and Antisocial Behavior Total scores of the at-risk sample were significantly different ($p < .001$) from those of the comparison sample, indicating poorer overall social-behavioral adjustment. Using Cohen's (1988) suggested method for determining practical meaning of group differences in mean scores, the ES estimates indicate the magnitude of these group differences to be large, ranging from approximately 1.58 to 1.72 standard deviations difference between score distributions of the two groups.

In addition to the contrasts of mean scores between the at-risk and comparison samples, the classification accuracy of HCSBS scores was evaluated by conducting a two-group linear discriminant function analysis, using the individual item-level HCSBS scores in a combined manner as a predictor variable, and group membership status of the entire sample (at-risk or comparison) as a grouping variable. The results of this analysis indicated that the social-behavioral ratings of the participants in the two groups predicted their group

Table 6.11. HCSBS total raw scores from the At-Risk and Comparison samples from the Merrell and Caldarella (1999) study, with means, standard deviations, analysis of variance (ANOVA) results, and effect size estimates

HCSBS scales	At-Risk		Comparison		F (1, 254)	ES
	M	SD	M	SD		
Social Competence Total	97.98	20.41	131.88	18.88	172.37*	1.72
Antisocial Behavior Total	87.17	27.38	51.5	17.64	137.39*	1.58

Key: *$p < .001$; ES, effect size; M, mean; SD, standard deviation.

membership in a statistically significant manner: Wilks' lambda = .33, chi-squared (65) = 220.12, $p < .001$. In terms of classification accuracy of the discriminant analysis, 92.37% of all participants were classified accurately into their respective group, including 92.0% of the at-risk sample and 92.9% of the comparison sample.

These results clearly support the validity of the HCSBS for one of its primary intended purposes. Based on this study, identification of children and youth who are at risk for a variety of negative outcomes is something that can be done efficiently and with a great deal of accuracy through the use of HCSBS scores.

Group Differences: Special Education Status

Lund and Merrell (2001) researched the construct validity of the HCSBS in terms of its ability to detect social-behavioral differences among parent ratings of 180 students ages 6–12 who had been identified for special education services in three service eligibility groups: learning disabilities (LD; $n = 60$), emotional-behavior disorders (EBD; $n = 60$), and a comparison sample of students in general education (GE; $n = 60$) who were not identified as having disabilities and did not receive special education services. Because prior research has shown that youth with LD and EBD would be expected to evidence poorer social-behavioral adjustment than students without disabilities, it was predicted that youth in the GE group would have significantly higher social competence and lower antisocial behavior ratings than youth in the LD and EBD groups and that the EBD group participants would have the poorest ratings of social-behavioral adjustment. Ratings for this study were selected from the HCSBS national norming sample using a randomized block procedure to ensure comparability between the groups with respect to all important variables except for the special education classification status. Each of the three groups included ratings of 38 boys and 22 girls.

Raw scores for the Social Competence Total and Antisocial Behavior Total scores were used for group comparison purposes. The scores of the three groups were compared and contrasted using a one-way ANOVA procedure, with follow-up pairwise contrasts using Scheffe's method for post-hoc analyses. In addition, ES estimates were calculated between all possible comparison pairs to help evaluate the practical meaning of score differences, based on Cohen's (1988) recommended procedure for ES estimation.

Means, standard deviations, and ANOVA results for this study are presented in Table 6.12. In addition, ES estimates for the pairwise contrasts of mean scores between the groups are presented in Table 6.13, along with the interpretive size of group differences based on Cohen's recommended interpretation guidelines. As predicted, the ANOVA was significant ($p < .001$), and follow-up pairwise contrasts indicated that the Social Competence Total and Antisocial Behavior Total scores of the three groups were all significantly different from each other. The HCSBS scores for the EBD group evidenced the poorest social-behavioral adjustment, the scores for the GE group evidenced

Table 6.12. HCSBS total raw scores for students with emotional-behavior disorders, students with learning disabilities, and students in general education from the Lund and Merrell (2001) study, with descriptive statistics and analysis of variance (ANOVA) results

HCSBS scales	EBD		LD		GE		F (2, 177)
	M	SD	M	SD	M	SD	
Social Competence Total	54.38[a]	23.04	67.53[b]	24.72	94.02[c]	22.73	44.23*
Antisocial Behavior Total	74.30[a]	25.59	49.02[b]	29.87	25.77[c]	21.40	52.89*

Note: For each row of data, pairs with differing superscript letters are significantly different at $p < .05$.

Key: *$p < .001$; EBD, emotional-behavior disorders; GE, general education; LD, learning disabilities; M, mean; SD, standard deviation.

the best social-behavioral adjustment, and the scores of the LD group were in between these two groups. As the ES estimate results in Table 6.13 indicate, each of the six pairwise contrasts produced meaningful effects, mostly large, ranging from .55 (slightly more than one half of a standard deviation difference between the pair of scores) to 2.07 (slightly more than 2 standard deviations difference between the pair of scores).

The results of the Lund and Merrell (2001) study demonstrate the ability of the HCSBS to detect differences in social competence and antisocial behavior of children and youth based on their status with respect to learning and emotional-behavior disorders. These group difference results support the validity of the HCSBS based on consequences of testing and its usefulness in classification. Because the HCSBS is purported to be useful as one component of an assessment battery for making classification and service eligibility decisions with respect to behavioral problems, these results are of particular importance in supporting the validity of the instrument for its intended uses.

Group Differences: ADHD Clinical Status

There is a great deal of research on impairments in social behavior of children with ADHD. In general, children with significant ADHD characteristics tend to have difficulty responding appropriately to others in social situations and tend to exhibit significant levels of problem behaviors, including antisocial

Table 6.13. Paired comparisons between HCSBS total scores for students with emotional-behavior disorders, students with learning disabilities, and students in general education from the Lund and Merrell (2001) study

Group contrasts	Effect size of mean HCSBS score comparisons	
	Social Competence Total	Antisocial Behavior Total
EBD/LD	.55 (medium)	.91 (large)
EBD/GE	1.73 (large)	2.07 (large)
LD/GE	1.12 (large)	.91 (large)

Key: EBD, emotional-behavior disorders; GE, general education; LD, learning disabilities.

behaviors (Barkley, 1997; Whalen & Henker, 1998). Because of the known social behavior problems that tend to accompany ADHD, it would be expected that a valid measure of social competence and antisocial behavior would distinguish clearly between children and youth with ADHD and comparison children and youth without ADHD. To that end, a validity study of the HCSBS was conducted by Merrell and Boelter (2001).

The sample for this study included parent ratings of 164 children ages 6–12 who were evaluated using the HCSBS. Half of the sample ($n = 82$) were children who had previously been identified by a mental health or medical professional as having ADHD, and the other half of the sample was a non-ADHD comparison group that was matched to the ADHD group in terms of age, gender, and ethnicity. Of the entire study sample, 80.5% were males, and 58.5% were Caucasian. These samples were developed from the HCSBS national norming sample using a randomized block selection design.

The HCSBS total raw scores of the two groups were contrasted using ANOVA and ES estimation procedures. The descriptive statistics for HCSBS scores, as well as the results of the analyses, are presented in Table 6.14. As these data indicate, the children in the ADHD group had significantly lower Social Competence scores and significantly higher Antisocial Behavior scores ($p < .001$) than the children in the non-ADHD comparison group. Furthermore, these differences were very large, with ES estimates indicating more than 2 standard deviations average difference between groups in terms of overlapping distributions of scores. In addition, a two-group linear discriminant function analysis was conducted, using the combined individual item scores from the HCSBS as a predictor variable and group membership as a grouping variable. The results of this analysis indicated that the social behavior ratings of participants predicted their group membership in a statistically significant manner: Wilks' lambda = .13, chi-squared (65) = 262.55, $p < .001$. An extremely high percentage (99.4%) of cases were correctly classified into their respective groups, including 98.8% (all but one) of the ADHD group, and 100% of the non-ADHD comparison group.

These results provide strong additional support for the HCSBS as a valid measure of social competence and antisocial behavior. Although this instrument was not developed specifically for the purpose of assessing ADHD, it is clear based on this study that the HCSBS may be a very useful tool for evaluating the social behavior characteristics of children and youth with this disorder.

Table 6.14. Means and standard deviations for HCSBS total scores for comparison groups of students with attention-deficit/hyperactivity disorder (ADHD) and students without ADHD (non-ADHD), with analysis of variance (ANOVA) results and effect size estimates

HCSBS scales	ADHD		Non-ADHD comparison		F (1, 254)	ES
	M	SD	M	SD		
Social Competence Total	53.36	17.97	94.21	19.78	133.36*	2.16
Antisocial Behavior Total	71.07	25.98	24.00	16.97	108.32*	2.19

Key: *$p < .001$; ES, effect size; M, mean; SD, standard deviation.

Group Differences: Gender

Extensive details regarding gender differences in HCSBS scores are presented in Chapter 4, in the discussion of development, standardization, and normative information. In review, significant differences between boys and girls have been found at all grade levels on both scales of the HCSBS. Within the HCSBS norming sample, girls as a group received from their parents or other informants higher ratings of social competence and lower ratings of antisocial behavior than boys as a group. The mean differences in score distributions for boys and girls in the norming sample average approximately one fourth to one third of a standard deviation, indicating meaningful but small ES estimates for both the Social Competence Total and Antisocial Behavior Total scores.

Although these modest but consistent differences do not justify the use of same-gender norms in most cases (for reasons explained in Chapter 4), they do provide additional supporting evidence for the validity of the HCSBS. A substantial body of evidence (see Merrell & Gimpel, 1998, for a review of the literature in this area) is consistent with these gender differences in social behavior ratings, and similar results have been found in other studies using large data sets. It is interesting to note that, on average, teacher ratings of child and adolescent social behavior tend to result in slightly larger gender differences in scores than do parent ratings. The HCSBS and SSBS-2 are consistent with regard to this pattern. Whereas the HCSBS norming sample contained differences of about one fourth to one third of a standard deviation in the Social Competence and Antisocial Behavior scores of boys and girls, these differences were closer to one half a standard deviation with the original SSBS norming group. In sum, the typical gender-based differences in social behavior ratings provide additional evidence of the validity of the HCSBS because these differences are consistent with theory and previous research.

SENSITIVITY TO TREATMENT OUTCOMES

A final type of validity evidence that has accumulated in support of the HCSBS is evidence of its sensitivity to treatment outcomes, or social-behavioral changes resulting from effective prevention and intervention programs. This type of validity evidence is somewhat difficult to categorize according to the organization of forms of validity in the *Standards*. Evidence of sensitivity to treatment outcomes may be considered as a type of validity evidence that is based on the outcomes of testing; however, in a strict sense, the characteristics measured in this type of study are really an outcome of intervention rather than an outcome of testing. Evidence of an assessment instrument's sensitivity to measuring changes in the construct of interest, following a procedure designed to produce such changes, would also be considered as evidence of construct validity. In any case, evidence of sensitivity to social behavior change resulting from treatment is an important component of demonstrating the validity of the HCSBS. Ideally, practitioners and researchers will use the HCSBS and SSBS-2 not only for screening and assessment, but also to assist in developing intervention plans and monitoring progress during intervention.

Two intervention studies where the HCSBS was used as a primary assessment tool to measure treatment outcomes are reviewed in this section. One of these studies was a multiyear effort aimed at preventing antisocial behavior, academic problems, and substance abuse in at-risk students from a general school population, whereas the other study was aimed at teaching anger management skills to inpatient youth who had been hospitalized in a psychiatric setting due to serious behavior and emotional problems. Both of these studies are reviewed in this section as evidence of the sensitivity of the HCSBS in measuring behavior change resulting from effective treatment.

Outcome Evidence: A Prevention Program

The HCSBS was used along with the SSBS-2 and a variety of other instruments as outcome measures for the *Prevention Plus* project, a multiyear prevention program aimed at decreasing prevalence rates of antisocial behavior, substance abuse, and gang membership among at-risk youth in Grades 6–9 in Ogden, Utah. In an article by West, Young, Mitchem, and Caldarella (1998) that provided an overview of the major findings from the Prevention Plus project, impressive behavioral, social, and academic gains were noted for the youth who participated.

The study included three groups: 1) a no-treatment group of 22 students who were referred by their principals for participation but did not participate in the prevention program, 2) a treatment group of 70 students who were judged to be at risk and who participated in the prevention program for 1 year, and 3) a treatment group of 80 students who were judged to be at risk and who participated in the prevention program for 2 years. Pre- and posttest measures, including the HCSBS (which was completed by parents of the students), were completed for all participants. The treatment group students received academic support, direct instruction for academic areas in which they were deficient, social skills training, and self-management training.

Among other outcomes, students who participated in the Prevention Plus program evidenced significant ($p < .01$) gains in SSBS-2 and HCSBS Social Competence scores, as well as significant ($p < .01$) decreases in SSBS-2 and HCSBS Antisocial Behavior scores. The Social Competence and Antisocial Behavior scores of the students in the no-treatment control group did not differ substantially from pretest to posttest and were significantly ($p < .01$) different at posttest (indicating poorer social skills and greater levels of problem behavior) from the scores of the project participants. It is interesting to note that participants in the 2-year treatment group (who were considered to have the highest risk levels at the onset of the project) showed the largest changes in social and antisocial behavior ratings.

The results of the Prevention Plus project provide compelling evidence not only for the positive results of the project but for the sensitivity of the HCSBS and SSBS-2 in detecting changes in social behavior that occurred as a result of the program. These findings are important because screening and assessment of at-risk youth and intervention planning and outcome evaluation are the primary purposes for which the HCSBS and SSBS-2 are purported to be useful.

Outcome Evidence: Anger Control Training

A study by Snyder, Kymissis, and Kessler (1999) included the HCSBS and SSBS-2 within a battery of assessment tools to measure the effectiveness of a brief group therapy intervention for adolescents with poor anger control. Participants in this study included 50 adolescents (28 males and 22 females) who had been admitted to a county psychiatric hospital in New York because of severe behavior, social, or emotional problems. The selection criteria for being included in this intervention study included 1) recommendations by a treatment team due to significant clinical indications of angry thoughts or feelings, disruptive behavior, and difficulty controlling anger and 2) a score of 75% or higher on the Trait Anger scale of the State-Trait Anger Expression Inventory (STAXI; Spielberger, 1988). Adolescent patients who met both of these criteria were randomly selected to either a treatment group or a control group, each of which included 25 youth.

The youth in the treatment group were involved in a group-based cognitive-behavioral anger management training intervention. This intervention was based on a scripted treatment manual and included four sessions that were delivered within a 2-week period. The focus of the four treatment sessions included a psychoeducational program to introduce the participants to anger management concepts, practice in specific cognitive and behavior strategies for responding adaptively to feelings of anger, engaging in role plays, receiving therapist and peer feedback on these role plays, and keeping daily "hassle logs." The youth in the control group were provided with an attention and education situation that involved the same number of sessions as the treatment group received but was not targeted specifically at teaching anger control strategies.

Following the intervention, teachers from the hospital's educational program (who were not involved in delivering the intervention) rated the adolescents using the Antisocial Behavior scale of the SSBS-2. Members of the hospital's nursing staff (who also were not involved in delivering the treatment) rated the adolescents using the Antisocial Behavior scale of the HCSBS. Both the teachers and the nursing staff rated the treatment group youth as exhibiting significantly lower ($p < .05$) rates of antisocial behavior than the control group youth. In terms of power analysis or standardized ES estimates, the strength of the difference between the two groups ranged from .39 for the teachers' SSBS ratings to .72 for the nurses' HCSBS ratings. Given the extensive efforts that were made to randomly assign the adolescents to the two groups (a computerized random selection procedure was used), the best explanation for the significant differences between the two groups is actual reductions of rates and intensity of antisocial behavior of the youth who were exposed to the cognitive-behavioral intervention. Thus, this study provides convincing evidence of the sensitivity of the HCSBS and SSBS-2 in measuring social behavior change resulting from treatment.

FUTURE RESEARCH

Although validity may be considered a unitary construct, validity evidence for specific purposes is not unitary—there are many ways to show such evidence. It is also important to consider that validation of a psychological or educational measure is an ongoing process. It is incorrect in most instances to consider a measure to be "validated." Rather, as evidence in support of its validity accrues, the validity base for a measure is strengthened. As specific types of validity evidence accumulate, the point may be reached where a measure may be considered to be valid for specific purposes. Thus, although the extensive evidence presented in this manual supports the validity of the HCSBS for particular purposes and under specific conditions, continued research is a valuable and necessary endeavor. Future research with the HCSBS will be conducted for the purpose of enhancing the base of validity evidence for specific uses of this scale.

SUMMARY

The HCSBS is purported to be a measure of social competence and antisocial behavior as these constructs are evidenced by children and youth in home and community settings. This chapter has included extensive evidence documenting the validity of the HCSBS for a variety of its intended purposes.

Using traditional validity terms, it may be stated that the HCSBS has strong evidence of content, construct, and criterion-related validity. Evidence based on test content, the internal structure of the scales, relations to other measures, and consequences of testing all indicate that the HCSBS is indeed a useful measure of social and antisocial behavior of children and youth. The accumulated validity evidence supports the use of the HCSBS for screening, assessment, classification, and intervention planning and monitoring of social and antisocial behavior of children and youth in home and community settings. Ongoing and future research efforts with the HCSBS and SSBS-2 will further establish the validity of these instruments for specific purposes.

REFERENCES

Achenbach, T.M. (1991). *Child Behavior Checklist for Ages 4–18.* Burlington: University of Vermont, Department of Psychiatry, Center for Children, Youth, and Families.

Achenbach, T.M., & Edelbrock, C.S. (1981). Behavioral problems and competencies reported by parents of normal and disturbed children aged four through sixteen. *Monographs for the Society for Research in Child Development, 46*(1, serial no. 188).

Achenbach, T.M., McConaughy, S.T., & Howell, C.T. (1987). Child/adolescent behavioral and emotional problems: Implications of cross-informant correlations for situational specificity. *Psychological Bulletin, 101,* 213–232.

American Educational Research Association (AERA), American Psychological Association (APA), & National Council on Measurement in Education (NCME). (1999). *Standards for educational and psychological testing.* Washington, DC: AERA.

American Psychiatric Association. (1994). *Diagnostic and statistical manual of mental disorders* (4th ed.). Washington, DC: Author.

American Psychiatric Association. (2000). *Diagnostic and statistical manual of mental disorders* (4th ed., Text Rev.). Washington, DC: Author.

Appelbaum, R.P., & Chambliss, W.J. (1997). *Sociology: A brief introduction.* New York: Longman.

Asher, S.R., & Taylor, A.R. (1981). The social outcomes of mainstreaming: Sociometric assessment and beyond. *Exceptional Children Quarterly, 1,* 13–30.

Barkley, R.A. (1997). *ADHD and the nature of self-control.* New York: Guilford.

Caldarella, P., & Merrell, K.W. (1997). Common dimensions of social skills of children and adolescents: A taxonomy of positive behaviors. *School Psychology Review, 26,* 265–279.

Chafouleas, S., Riley-Tilman, T.C., & Sugai, G. (2007). *School-based behavioral assessment: Informing intervention and instruction.* New York: Guilford.

Cohen, J. (1988). *Statistical power analysis in the behavioral sciences* (2nd ed.). Mahwah, NJ: Lawrence Erlbaum Associates.

Coie, J.D., Dodge, K.A., & Cappotelli, H. (1982). Dimensions and types of social status: A cross-age perspective. *Developmental Psychology, 18,* 557–570.

Conners, C.K. (1997). *Conners Rating Scale System–Revised.* North Tonawanda, NY: Multi-Health Systems.

Conners, C.K., & Werry, J.S. (1979). Pharmacotherapy. In H.C. Quay & J.S. Werry (Eds.), *Psychopathological disorders of childhood* (2nd ed.). New York: John Wiley & Sons.

Connolly, J. (1983). A review of sociometric procedures in the assessment of social competence in children. *Applied Research in Mental Retardation, 4,* 315–317.

Cowen, E.L., Pederson, A., Babigan, H., Izzo, L.D., & Trost, M.A. (1973). Long-term follow-up of early detected vulnerable children. *Journal of Consulting and Clinical Psychology, 41,* 438–446.

Cronbach, L. (1951). Coefficient alpha and the internal structure of tests. *Psychometrika, 16,* 297–334.

Cronbach, L. (1990). *Essentials of psychological testing* (5th ed.). New York: Harper & Row.

Crone, D.A., & Horner, R.H. (2003). *Building positive behavior support systems in schools: Functional behavioral assessment.* New York: Guilford.

Cullinan, D., Epstein, M.H., & Kauffman, J.M. (1984). Teacher's ratings of students' behaviors: What constitutes behavior disorder in schools? *Behavioral Disorders, 10,* 9–19.

REFERENCES

Dillon, J.A., Michael, K.D., & Huelsman, J.A. (2001, August). *Social competence and delinquency: The role of psychopathic traits*. Paper presented at the meeting of the American Psychological Association, San Francisco.

Dodge, K., Coie, J., & Brakke, N. (1982). Behavior patterns of socially rejected and neglected adolescents: The roles of social approach and aggression. *Journal of Abnormal Child Psychology, 10,* 389–410.

Fan, X., Wilson, V.L., & Kapes, J.T. (1996). Ethnic group representation in test construction samples and test bias: The standardization fallacy revisited. *Educational and Psychological Measurement, 56,* 365–381.

Foster, S.L., & Ritchey, W.L. (1979). Issues in the assessment of social competence in children. *Journal of Applied Behavior Analysis, 12,* 625–638.

Frick, P.J., Bodin, B., & Barry, C.T. (2000). Psychopathic traits and conduct problems in community and clinic-referred samples of children: Further development of the Psychopathy Screening Device. *Psychological Assessment, 12,* 382–393.

Gorsuch, R.L. (1997). Exploratory factor analysis: Its role in item analysis. *Journal of Personality Assessment, 68,* 532–560.

Gregory, R.J. (2000). *Psychological testing: History, principles, and applications* (3rd ed.). Boston: Allyn & Bacon.

Gresham, F.M. (1986). Conceptual issues in the assessment of social competence in children. In P. Strain, M.J. Guralnick, & H.M. Walker (Eds.), *Children's social behavior: Development, assessment, and modification* (pp. 143–179). San Diego: Academic Press.

Gresham, F.M., & Elliott, S.N. (1990). *Social Skills Rating System*. Circle Pines, MN: American Guidance Service.

Gresham, F.M., & Reschly, D.J. (1987). Dimensions of social competence: Method factors in the assessment of adaptive behavior, social skills, and peer acceptance. *Journal of School Psychology, 25,* 367–381.

Holland, M.L., Gimpel, G.A., & Merrell, K.W. (2001). *ADHD Symptoms Rating Scale*. Wilmington, DE: Wide Range.

Hops, H. (1983). Children's social competence and skill: Current research practices and future directions. *Behavior Therapy, 14,* 3–18.

Horner, R.H., & Carr, E.G. (1997) Behavioral support for students with severe disabilities: Functional assessment and comprehensive intervention. *Journal of Special Education, 31,* 84–109.

Individuals with Disabilities Education Act Amendments (IDEA) of 1997, PL 105-17, 20 U.S.C. §§ 1400 *et seq.*

Individuals with Disabilities Education Act (IDEA) of 1990, PL 101-476, 20 U.S.C. §§ 1400 *et seq.*

Kauffman, J.M. (2000). *Characteristics of emotional and behavioral disorders of children and youth* (7th ed.). Columbus, OH: Merrill/Prentice-Hall.

Kazdin, A.E. (1979). Situational specificity: The two-edged sword of behavioral assessment. *Behavioral Assessment, 1,* 57–75.

Kerr, M.M., & Nelson, C.M. (1989). *Strategies for managing behavior problems in the classroom* (2nd ed.). Columbus, OH: Merrill.

Kohn, M.L., & Schooler, C. (1983). *Work and personality: An inquiry into the impact of social stratification*. Norwood, NJ: Ablex.

Landau, S., & Milich, R. (1990). Assessment of children's social status and peer relations. In A.M. LaGreca (Ed.), *Through the eyes of a child* (pp. 259–291). Boston: Allyn & Bacon.

Loeber, R. (1985). Patterns of development of antisocial child behavior. *Annals of Child Development, 2,* 77–116.

Lund, J., & Merrell, K.W. (2001). Social and antisocial behavior of children with learning and behavior disorders: Construct validity of the Home and Community Social Behavior Scales. *Journal of Psychoeducational Assessment, 19,* 112–122.

McComas, J.J., Hoch, H., & Mace, F.C. (2000). Functional analysis. In E.S. Shapiro & T.R. Kratochwill (Eds.), *Conducting school-based assessments of child and adolescent behavior* (pp. 78–101). New York: Guilford.

Meichenbaum, D., Butler, L., & Gruson, L. (1981). Toward a conceptual model of social competence. In J.D. Wyne & M.D. Smye (Eds.), *Social competence*. New York: Guilford.

Merrell, K.W. (2000a). Informant report: Rating scale measures. In E.S. Shapiro & T.R. Kratochwill (Eds.), *Conducting school-based assessment of child and adolescent behaviors* (pp. 203–234). New York: Guilford.

Merrell, K.W. (2000b). Informant report: Theory and research in using child behavior rating scales in school settings. In E.S. Shapiro & T.R. Kratochwill (Eds.), *Behavioral assessment in schools* (2nd ed., pp. 233–256). New York: Guilford.

Merrell, K.W. (2002). *School Social Behavior Scales, Second Edition user's guide*. Baltimore: Paul H. Brookes Publishing Co.

Merrell, K.W. (2008). *Behavioral, social, and emotional assessment of children and adolescents* (3rd ed.). New York: Taylor and Francis/Routledge.

Merrell, K.W., & Boelter, E.W. (2001). An investigation of relationships between social behavior and ADHD in children and youth: Construct validity of the Home and Community Social Behavior Scales. *Journal of Emotional and Behavioral Disorders, 9,* 260–269.

Merrell, K.W., & Caldarella, P. (1999). Social-behavioral assessment of at-risk early adolescent students: Validity of a parent report form of the School Social Behavior Scales. *Journal of Psychoeducational Assessment, 17,* 36–49.

Merrell, K.W., Caldarella, P., Streeter, A.L., Boelter, E.W., & Gentry, A. (2001). Convergent validity of the Home and Community Social Behavior Scales: Comparisons with five behavior rating scales. *Psychology in the Schools, 38,* 313–325.

Merrell, K.W., & Crowley, S.L. (2000, August). *Factor structure of the Home and Community Social Behavior Scales*. Paper presented at the meeting of the American Psychological Association, Washington, D.C.

Merrell, K.W., Ervin, R.A., & Gimpel, G.A. (2006). *School psychology for the 21st century: Foundations and practices*. New York: Guilford.

Merrell, K.W., & Gimpel, G.A. (1998). *Social skills of children and adolescents: Conceptualization, assessment, treatment*. Mahwah, NJ: Lawrence Erlbaum Associates.

Michael, K.D., Dillon, J.A., & Huelsman, T.J. (2001, August). *Parenting and antisocial behaviors: Do personality variables make a difference?* Paper presented at the meeting of the American Psychological Association, San Francisco.

Mischel, W. (1968). *Personality and assessment*. New York: John Wiley & Sons.

Mueller, E. (1979). (Toddlers + toys) = (An autonomous social system). In M. Lewis & L.A. Rosenbaum (Eds.), *The child and its family* (pp. 169–194). New York: Plenum.

Peacock Hill Working Group. (1991). Problems and promises in special education and related services for children and youth with emotional or behavioral disorders. *Behavioral Disorders, 16,* 299–313.

Reynolds, C.R., & Kamphaus, R.W. (1992). *Behavior Assessment System for Children*. Circle Pines, MN: American Guidance Service.

Roff, M., Sells, B., & Golden, M. (1972). *Social adjustment and personality development in children*. Minneapolis: University of Minnesota Press.

Salvia, J., & Ysseldyke, J.E. (2000). *Assessment* (8th ed.). Boston: Houghton-Mifflin.

Snyder, K.V., Kymissis, P., & Kessler, K. (1999). Anger management for adolescents: Efficacy of brief group therapy. *Journal of the American Academy of Child and Adolescent Psychiatry, 38,* 1409–1416.

Spielberger, C.D. (1988). *State-Trait Anger Expression Inventory*. Redwood City, CA: Mind Garden.

Stanley, E.D., & Baca-Zinn, M. (1997). *Social problems*. (7th ed.) Boston: Allyn & Bacon.

U.S. Census Bureau, Population Estimates Program, Population Division. (2001, July 2). *Resident population estimates of the United States by sex, race, and Hispanic origin: Short-term projection to July 1, 2000.* Washington, DC: Author.

U.S. Department of Education, National Center for Education Statistics. (2000). Children 0–21 years old served in federally supported programs for the disabled, by type of disability: 1976–77 to 1997–98. *Digest of Education Statistics.* Available online at http://nces.ed.gov/pubs2000/Digest99/d99t053.html

Walker, H.M., Gresham, F.M., & Ramsey, E. (2004). *Antisocial behavior in school: Evidence-based practices* (2nd ed.). New York: Wadsworth.

Walker, H.M., & Hops, H. (1976). Increasing academic achievement by reinforcing direct academic performance and/or facilitating nonacademic responses. *Journal of Educational Psychology, 68,* 218–225.

Walker, H.M., McConnell, S.R., & Clarke, J.Y. (1985). Social skills training in school settings: A model for the social integration of handicapped children into less restrictive settings. In R. McMahon & R.D. Peters (Eds.), *Childhood disorders: Behavioral-developmental approaches* (pp. 140–168). New York: Brunner/Mazel.

Watson, T.S., & Steege, M.R. (2003). *Conducting school-based functional behavioral assessments: A practitioner's guide.* New York: Guilford.

West, R.P., Young, K.R., Mitchem, K.J., & Caldarella, P. (1998, Winter). What's happening in Utah to help students at risk for antisocial behavior? *CPD News, 21*(2). Logan: Utah State University, Center for Persons with Disabilities.

Whalen, C.K., & Henker, B. (1998). Attention deficit/hyperactivity disorder. In T.H. Ollendick & M. Hersen (Eds.), *Handbook of child psychopathology* (3rd ed.). New York: Plenum.

Worthen, B.R., Borg, W.R., Caldarella, & White, K.R. (1993). *Measurement and evaluation in the schools: A practical guide.* White Plains, NY: Longman.

SCORE CONVERSION TABLES FOR AGES 5-11

HCSBS
SOCIAL COMPETENCE SCALE

Table A.1

Score Conversion Table for
Peer Relations Subscale for Ages 5–11

Raw Score	T-Score	Percentile Rank	Raw Score	T-Score	Percentile Rank	Raw Score	T-Score	Percentile Rank
17–22	12	<1	50	38	12	69	52	52
23–26	17	<1	51	38	13	70	53	55
27–28	20	1	52	39	15	71	54	58
29–31	21	1	53	40	17	72	55	61
32–33	24	2	54	41	18	73	55	66
34	25	3	55	41	20	74	56	70
35	26	3	56	42	21	75	57	73
36	27	3	57	43	23	76	58	77
37–38	28	4	58	44	25	77	58	80
39	29	4	59	44	27	78	59	83
40	30	4	60	45	30	79	60	86
41	31	5	61	46	33	80	61	88
42	31	6	62	47	35	81	61	90
43	32	7	63	48	39	82	62	92
44	33	7	64	48	40	83	63	95
45–46	34	8	65	49	42	84	64	97
47	35	9	66	50	47	85	65	99
48	36	10	67	51	48			
49	37	11	68	51	50			

Descriptive Statistics for Raw Scores: $M = 66.16$, $SD = 12.96$

Social Functioning Levels

Raw Score Range	Social Functioning Level
17–40	High Risk
41–54	At-Risk
55–77	Average
78–85	High Functioning

HCSBS

SOCIAL COMPETENCE SCALE

Table A.2

Score Conversion Table for
Self-Management/Compliance Subscale for Ages 5–11

Raw Score	T-Score	Percentile Rank
15-17	16	< 1
18-22	18	< 1
23-24	23	1
25	24	1
26-27	25	2
28-29	27	3
30	29	3
31	29	4
32	30	5
33	31	6
34	32	7
35	33	7
36	34	8
37	35	8
38	36	10
39	36	11
40	37	12

Raw Score	T-Score	Percentile Rank
41	38	13
42	39	16
43	40	17
44	41	20
45	42	22
46	43	24
47	43	27
48	44	28
49	45	31
50	46	33
51	47	36
52	48	39
53	49	43
54	49	45
55	50	48
56	51	52
57	52	55

Raw Score	T-Score	Percentile Rank
58	53	58
59	54	60
60	55	64
61	56	68
62	56	71
63	57	75
64	58	78
65	59	81
66	60	85
67	61	88
68	62	90
69	63	93
70	63	95
71	64	97
72	65	98
73	66	98
74-75	68	99

Descriptive Statistics for Raw Scores: $M = 54.60$, $SD = 11.50$

Social Functioning Levels

Raw Score Range	Social Functioning Level
15-31	High Risk
32-43	At-Risk
44-64	Average
65-75	High Functioning

Table A.3

Score Conversion Table for
Social Competence Total Score for Ages 5–11

Raw Score	T-Score	Percentile Rank	Raw Score	T-Score	Percentile Rank	Raw Score	T-Score	Percentile Rank
32	12	< 1	87-89	36	10	125-126	52	52
33-41	16	< 1	90-91	37	12	127-128	53	55
42-56	22	1	92-93	38	12	129-131	54	60
57	23	1	94-96	39	15	132-133	55	65
58-59	24	1	97-98	40	18	134-135	56	67
60-63	25	1	99-100	41	19	136-138	57	72
64	26	2	101-103	42	21	139-140	58	77
65-67	27	3	104-105	43	23	141-142	59	81
68-70	28	3	106-107	44	26	143-145	60	85
71-72	29	4	108-110	45	28	146-147	61	88
73-75	30	5	111-112	46	32	148-149	62	92
76-77	31	6	113-114	47	34	150-152	63	94
78-79	32	6	115-117	48	38	153-154	64	96
80-82	33	7	118-119	49	42	155-156	65	98
83-84	34	8	120-121	50	46	157-158	66	99
85-86	35	9	122-124	51	49	159-160	67	99

Descriptive Statistics for Raw Scores: $M = 120.77$, $SD = 23.32$

Social Functioning Levels

Raw Score Range	Social Functioning Level
32-72	High Risk
73-100	At-Risk
101-140	Average
141-160	High Functioning

Table A.4

Score Conversion Table for
Defiant/Disruptive Subscale for Ages 5–11

Raw Score	T-Score	Percentile Rank	Raw Score	T-Score	Percentile Rank	Raw Score	T-Score	Percentile Rank
15	36	2	32	50	61	49	65	93
16	36	4	33	51	64	50-51	66	94
17	37	8	34	52	66	52	68	95
18	38	10	35	53	69	53	69	96
19	39	13	36	54	71	54	70	96
20	40	17	37	55	73	55-56	70	97
21	41	21	38	56	75	57-58	73	97
22	42	24	39	57	77	59	74	97
23	43	29	40	57	78	60-61	75	98
24	43	32	41	58	80	62-63	77	98
25	44	36	42	59	83	64	78	98
26	45	39	43	60	84	65	79	99
27	46	42	44	61	87	66	80	99
28	47	45	45	62	89	67-69	81	>99
29	48	50	46	63	90	70-71	84	>99
30	49	53	47	63	91	72-75	85	>99
31	50	58	48	64	92			

Descriptive Statistics for Raw Scores: $M = 31.55$, $SD = 11.46$

Social Functioning Levels

Raw Score Range	Social Functioning Level
15-41	Average
42-52	At-Risk
53-75	High Risk

Table A.5

Score Conversion Table for
Antisocial/Aggressive Subscale for Ages 5–11

Raw Score	T-Score	Percentile Rank	Raw Score	T-Score	Percentile Rank	Raw Score	T-Score	Percentile Rank
17	40	7	33	55	79	49	71	95
18	41	14	34	56	81	50	72	96
19	42	21	35	57	82	51	73	96
20	43	27	36	58	84	52	74	96
21	44	36	37	59	85	53	75	97
22	45	43	38	60	87	54	76	97
23	46	49	39	61	89	55-56	77	97
24	47	52	40	62	90	57-58	78	97
25	48	56	41	63	91	59-60	80	98
26	49	59	42	64	92	61	82	98
27	50	64	43	65	92	62-63	83	98
28	51	67	44	66	93	64	85	99
29	52	70	45	67	93	65-68	86	99
30	53	73	46	68	94	69-70	90	99
31	53	76	47	69	95	71-75	92	>99
32	54	78	48	70	95	76-85	97	>99

Descriptive Statistics for Raw Scores: *M* = 27.37, *SD* = 10.41

Social Functioning Levels

Raw Score Range	Social Functioning Level
17-33	Average
34-49	At-Risk
50-85	High Risk

Table A.6
Score Conversion Table for Antisocial Behavior Total Score for Ages 5–11

Raw Score	T-Score	Percentile Rank	Raw Score	T-Score	Percentile Rank	Raw Score	T-Score	Percentile Rank
32	37	2	67-68	54	73	102-103	71	95
33-34	38	4	69-70	55	75	104-105	72	96
35-36	39	8	71-72	56	77	106-108	73	96
37-38	40	11	73-74	57	80	109-111	74	96
39-40	41	16	75-76	58	82	112-113	76	97
41-43	42	24	77-78	59	83	114-116	77	97
44-45	43	31	79-80	60	85	117-118	78	98
46-47	44	36	81-83	61	87	119-120	79	98
48-49	45	39	84-85	62	89	121-123	80	99
50-51	46	43	86-87	63	91	124-125	81	99
52-53	47	47	88-89	64	92	126-129	83	99
54-55	48	53	90-91	65	92	130-132	85	99
56-57	49	55	92-93	66	93	133-135	86	> 99
58-59	50	60	94-95	67	93	136-138	87	> 99
60-61	51	64	96-97	68	94	140-160	89	> 99
62-64	52	69	98-99	69	95			
65-66	53	72	100-101	70	95			

Descriptive Statistics for Raw Scores: $M = 58.92$, $SD = 21.07$

Social Functioning Levels

Raw Score Range	Social Functioning Level
32-74	Average
75-103	At-Risk
104-160	High Risk

SCORE CONVERSION TABLES FOR AGES 12-18   B

HCSBS

SOCIAL COMPETENCE SCALE

Table B.1

Score Conversion Table for
Peer Relations Subscale for Ages 12–18

Raw Score	T-Score	Percentile Rank	Raw Score	T-Score	Percentile Rank	Raw Score	T-Score	Percentile Rank
17-21	11	<1	49	35	9	67	49	42
22-24	13	<1	50	36	10	68	50	44
25-26	15	<1	51	36	11	69	51	46
27-31	16	1	52	37	12	70	52	48
32	21	1	53	38	13	71	52	52
33	22	1	54	39	14	72	53	56
34	23	2	55	40	15	73	54	60
35-36	24	2	56	40	17	74	55	62
37	25	2	57	41	18	75	56	66
38	26	3	58	42	19	76	56	70
39	27	4	59	43	21	77	57	75
40-41	28	4	60	44	25	78	58	79
42	29	4	61	44	28	79	59	82
43	30	5	62	45	30	80	60	85
44	31	5	63	46	32	81	60	87
45	32	6	64	47	34	82	61	91
46	32	7	65	48	37	83	62	95
47	33	8	66	48	40	84	63	97
48	34	8				85	64	99

Descriptive Statistics for Raw Scores: *M* = 68.05, *SD* = 12.48

Social Functioning Levels

Raw Score Range	Social Functioning Level
17-42	High Risk
43-58	At-Risk
59-78	Average
79-85	High Functioning

Table B.2

Score Conversion Table for Self-Management/Compliance Subscale for Ages 12–18

Raw Score	T-Score	Percentile Rank
15-19	17	<1
20-21	18	1
22-24	19	1
25-26	22	1
27	24	1
28	25	2
29	26	2
30	27	2
31-32	28	3
33	29	4
34	30	5
35	31	6
36	32	6
37	33	7
38	34	8
39	34	9
40	35	9

Raw Score	T-Score	Percentile Rank
41	36	10
42	37	13
43	38	14
44	39	16
45	40	17
46	40	18
47	41	21
48	42	23
49	43	25
50	44	27
51	45	29
52	46	31
53	47	33
54	47	35
55	48	39
56	49	41
57	50	44

Raw Score	T-Score	Percentile Rank
58	51	48
59	52	51
60	53	54
61	53	59
62	54	62
63	55	66
64	56	69
65	57	73
66	58	78
67	59	81
68	60	84
69	60	88
70	61	91
71	62	93
72	63	95
73	64	97
74	65	98
75	66	99

Descriptive Statistics for Raw Scores: $M = 56.99$, $SD = 11.55$

Social Functioning Levels

Raw Score Range	Social Functioning Level
15-33	High Risk
34-46	At-Risk
47-66	Average
67-75	High Functioning

Table B.3

Score Conversion Table for Social Competence Total Score for Ages 12–18

Raw Score	T-Score	Percentile Rank	Raw Score	T-Score	Percentile Rank	Raw Score	T-Score	Percentile Rank
32-44	14	<1	86-87	33	7	124-126	50	44
45-47	16	<1	88-89	34	9	127-128	51	48
48-53	18	<1	90	35	10	129-130	52	51
54-55	19	1	91-94	36	11	131-132	53	55
56	20	1	95-96	37	12	133-135	54	60
57-59	21	1	97-98	38	13	136-137	55	64
60-61	22	1	99-101	39	15	138-139	56	68
62-64	23	2	102-103	40	16	140-142	57	72
65-66	24	2	104-105	41	17	143-144	58	78
67-68	25	2	106-107	42	21	145-146	59	81
69-70	26	2	108-110	43	23	147-148	60	85
71-73	27	3	111-112	44	26	149	61	90
74-75	28	4	113-114	45	28	150-151	61	92
76-78	29	4	115-116	46	30	152-153	62	94
79-80	30	5	117-119	47	33	154-155	63	95
81-82	31	6	120-121	48	37	156-157	64	98
83-85	32	7	122-123	49	40	158-160	65	99

Descriptive Statistics for Raw Scores: $M = 125.04$, $SD = 22.78$

Social Functioning Levels

Raw Score Range	Social Functioning Level
32-78	High Risk
79-105	At-Risk
106-144	Average
145-160	High Functioning

HCSBS

Table B.4

Score Conversion Table for
Defiant/Disruptive Subscale for Ages 12–18

Raw Score	T-Score	Percentile Rank	Raw Score	T-Score	Percentile Rank	Raw Score	T-Score	Percentile Rank
15	38	4	34	54	74	54	71	96
16	39	8	35	55	75	55	72	96
17	40	13	36	56	77	56	73	96
18	41	17	37	57	78	57	74	96
19	41	21	38	58	80	58	75	97
20	42	27	39	58	82	59	75	98
21	43	32	40	59	84	60	76	98
22	44	35	41	60	86	61	77	98
23	45	39	42	61	87	62	78	99
24	46	45	43	62	88	63-64	79	99
25	46	48	44	63	89	65-66	80	99
26	47	51	45-46	64	90	67-68	81	99
27	48	56	47	65	91	69-70	85	99
28	49	58	48	66	92	71-72	86	> 99
29	50	61	49	67	94	73	87	> 99
30	51	64	50	68	94	74	88	> 99
31	52	66	51	69	94	75	89	> 99
32	52	69	52	69	95			
33	53	72	53	70	95			

Descriptive Statistics for Raw Scores: $M = 29.13$, $SD = 11.74$

Social Functioning Levels

Raw Score Range	Social Functioning Level
15-38	Average
39-53	At-Risk
54-75	High Risk

HCSBS

ANTISOCIAL BEHAVIOR SCALE

Table B.5

Score Conversion Table for
Antisocial/Aggressive Subscale for Ages 12–18

Raw Score	T-Score	Percentile Rank	Raw Score	T-Score	Percentile Rank	Raw Score	T-Score	Percentile Rank
17	41	11	35	58	83	55	76	98
18	42	17	36	59	84	56	77	98
19	43	27	37	60	85	57	78	98
20	44	36	38-39	61	87	58	79	98
21	45	44	40	62	89	59	80	98
22	46	50	41	63	90	60	81	98
23	47	54	42	64	90	61-62	82	99
24	48	59	43	65	91	63	84	99
25	48	63	44	66	92	64-66	85	99
26	49	65	45	67	93	67-68	87	99
27	50	68	46	68	94	69-71	88	99
28	51	71	47	69	95	72-73	92	99
29	52	73	48	70	95	74-77	93	>99
30	53	75	49	71	96	78-81	98	>99
31	54	77	50	72	96	82-84	101	>99
32	55	78	51-52	73	97	85	104	>99
33	56	80	53	74	97			
34	57	82	54	75	97			

Descriptive Statistics for Raw Scores: $M = 26.65$, $SD = 10.78$

Social Functioning Levels

Raw Score Range	Social Functioning Level
17-33	Average
34-48	At-Risk
49-85	High Risk

Table B.6
Score Conversion Table for Antisocial Behavior Total Score for Ages 12–18

Raw Score	T-Score	Percentile Rank	Raw Score	T-Score	Percentile Rank	Raw Score	T-Score	Percentile Rank
32	39	3	68-69	56	77	105-106	73	96
33-34	40	7	70-72	57	80	107-109	74	97
35-37	41	14	73-74	58	83	110-111	75	97
38-39	42	22	75-76	59	84	112-113	76	98
40-41	43	29	77-78	60	86	114-115	77	98
42-43	44	34	79-80	61	87	116-117	78	98
44-45	45	40	81-82	62	88	118-119	79	98
46-48	46	48	83-85	63	89	120-122	80	99
49-50	47	53	86-87	64	90	123-124	81	99
51-52	48	56	88-89	65	91	125-131	85	99
53-54	49	59	90-91	66	92	132-140	89	99
55-56	50	62	92-93	67	93	141-142	90	99
57-58	51	65	94-95	68	94	143-147	92	>99
59-61	52	68	96-98	69	94	148-149	93	>99
62-63	53	71	99-100	70	95	150-152	94	>99
64-65	54	74	101-102	71	96	153-160	98	>99
66-67	55	76	103-104	72	96			

Descriptive Statistics for Raw Scores: $M = 55.77$, $SD = 21.80$

Social Functioning Levels

Raw Score Range	Social Functioning Level
32-72	Average
73-98	At-Risk
99-160	High Risk